HISTORY™

THIS DAY IN
HISTORY
for KIDS

1,001 REMARKABLE MOMENTS & FASCINATING FACTS

DAN BOVA

ILLUSTRATIONS *by* **RUSSELL SHAW**

kids
HEARST
HOME

JANUARY
8

FEBRUARY
25

MARCH
41

DECEMBER
201

NOVEMBER
181

OCTOBER
163

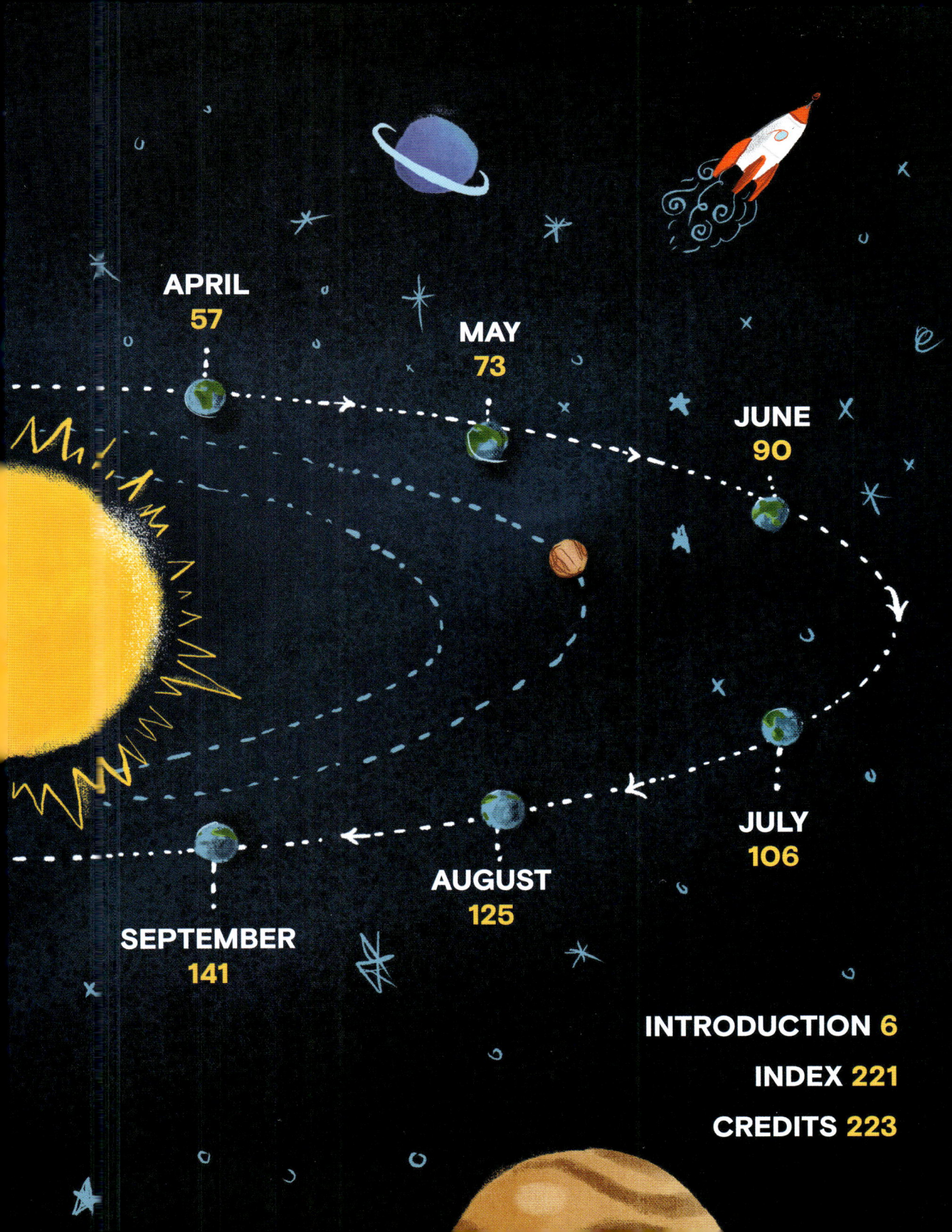

APRIL
57

MAY
73

JUNE
90

JULY
106

AUGUST
125

SEPTEMBER
141

INTRODUCTION 6

INDEX 221

CREDITS 223

INTRODUCTION

WHAT IN THE WORLD HAPPENED Today?

WE'RE GLAD YOU ASKED BECAUSE THAT'S WHAT YOU'RE ABOUT TO FIND OUT! The pages of this book are packed with fascinating, astonishing, and incredible events that happened on every single day of the year. And as you'll see, history is very, very busy.

Tons of epic events happened on the same day but in different years. Sometimes it makes sense, like June 28. On that day in 1914, the event that sparked World War I occurred, and exactly five years later, on June 28, 1919, a treaty was signed that would bring about its end.

But other times, it is totally random. Like February 5, for example: On that day in 1869, **the world's largest gold nugget was found** (167 pounds!), and also on that day in 1953, England finally ended its World War II–era candy rationing. (Actually, when you think about it, they are kind of related—both events are pretty sweet!)

So why look at history? Because it can be fun and inspiring. Remember, you can't spell history without *story* and there are tons of mind-blowing ones in here. You're going to learn about amazing inventors, incredible leaders, and wild daredevils who not only dreamed of doing the impossible but did it!

There's another reason to know about the past. You've probably heard the expression "Those who don't learn from history are doomed to repeat it," but what does that mean exactly? Here's a simple way to think of it. Say it is a steamy summer day and your friend offers you a cup of **broccoli-flavored ice cream.** You take a spoonful and instantly spit it out. Nasty! Then the next day, it's crazy hot again and your friend offers you *another* cup of broccoli-flavored ice cream. If you don't learn from yesterday's experience, you're doomed to gag again. Get it?

Yes, that is a very simplistic (and gross) explanation, but to be serious for a second, at times this book is going to discuss historical events that are terrible and horrifying. And the reason they're included is because it is vitally important to recognize the mistakes and troubling patterns that led to these tragedies so that we can do our best to make sure they never happen again.

Now back to the fun stuff: As you flip around, be sure to fill in your own historical moments at the end of each month. Yes, it is OK to write inside this book! You might write about birthdays, awesome trips you went on, or the day you learned to ride a bike—anything! This book won't only teach you about history, it will also become your own personal time capsule. Who knows, future historians may find it one day and proclaim a new holiday on the day you decided not to eat broccoli ice cream!

JANUARY 1

NEW YEAR'S DAY. Keep your room clean, exercise more, eat less junk food... Why do we tend to start off each year promising to do a bummer list of tasks and chores? You can thank the ancient Babylonians, who made the first known New Year's resolutions 4,000 years ago. Did kids procrastinate doing homework back then too?

1863 ● Nearing the third year of the Civil War, **President Abraham Lincoln issues the Emancipation Proclamation**, which frees enslaved people within the rebellious areas.

1892 ● Ellis Island in New York Harbor opens as an inspection station for incoming immigrants. A teenager from Ireland named Annie Moore and her two little brothers are the first to come through. More than 12 million people follow Annie over the next 62 years. Welcome to America!

1959 ● The Cuban Revolution results in corrupt dictator Fulgencio Batista being forced to flee the country by Fidel Castro. Batista lives out the rest of his life in Spain with the $300 million fortune he escaped with, and Castro begins a five-decade rule that severely limits citizens' freedoms.

2002 ● **The Euro goes into public circulation**, eventually becoming the one currency in 19 different European countries.

Here's how to say, "What a rip-off" in three different languages:

FRENCH *Quelle arnaque!*
GERMAN *Was für eine Abzocke!*
SPANISH *¡Vaya timo!*

1920 • It's the birthday of famous sci-fi author Isaac Asimov, which is why it's also National Science Fiction Day. Read a space adventure or start an intergalactic war to celebrate!

1975 • Amateur biologist Kenneth Brugger discovers a remote spot in Mexico that is covered with millions of monarch butterflies. Until that point, scientists did not know where the fluttery creatures disappeared to every winter. Every year, monarchs make a 3,000-mile trip from the U.S. and Canada to escape the cold...and take a well-deserved rest. Their wings gotta be tired after that!

2004 • **NASA's *Stardust* space probe makes an extremely close flyby to Comet Wild 2.** It is the first spacecraft to capture dust from a comet's wake. And presumably, the first spacecraft to sneeze.

JANUARY 3

1888 • **Inventor Marvin Stone patents the paper drinking straw.** Thank him the next time you slurp a cool drink on a hot day.

❓ Did You Know?

A patent is an official document that says you invented something, and no one is allowed to copy it for a set amount of time.

What Is the Far Side of the Moon?

Since the moon rotates at the exact same rate as it revolves around the earth, we get to see only one side of it when we look up. It wasn't until the Soviet Union sent the *Luna 3* probe up in 1959 that we got a peak at the moon's backside (which seems pretty rude when you think about it).

2019 • **China's *Chang'e-4* spacecraft is the first to land on the far side of the moon.**

JANUARY 4

1809
Louis Braille is born. The French educator, who was blinded at age 3, invented the Braille system, which allows blind people to read using their sense of touch.

2010
The Burj Khalifa building officially opens in Dubai. At 2,716.5 feet high, it is the tallest building in the world. If you plan on visiting and want to see the amazing view from the top, we suggest taking the elevator and avoiding the stairs.

★ It's National Spaghetti Day!

WHO INVENTED SPAGHETTI? This question is harder than chewing a box of uncooked linguine. There is a popular belief that explorer Marco Polo brought noodles back to Italy after his travels in China, but Massimo Montanari, author of *A Short History of Spaghetti With Tomato Sauce*, says that's a meatball-size myth. He writes that dried noodles were first introduced to people on the Italian island of Sicily by Arab conquerors and were being manufactured there by the 12th century. Ever since then, Italy has become the pasta capital of the world.

JANUARY  5

❓ Did You Know?

Although the Golden Gate Bridge is called golden, its official color, named by designer Irving F. Morrow, is International Orange.

1919
The Curse of the Bambino begins when the five-time World Series champion Boston Red Sox sell Babe Ruth's contract to the New York Yankees. The Red Sox didn't win another World Series until 2004, 86 years later. That was one heck of a curse!

1933
Construction starts on the iconic Golden Gate Bridge. When it is finished in 1937, it becomes the tallest and longest suspension bridge in the world. While it is no longer the record holder (nearly 20 bridges are bigger), it is still without a doubt the coolest looking.

1941
Ponyo's papa is born! Legendary Japanese animation director Hayao Miyazaki also made *Spirited Away*, *Howl's Moving Castle*, and a ton of other awesomely artistic films. And unlike Pixar, Miyazaki's movies are all drawn by hand—there can be more than 100,000 drawings per flick.

ORANGE YOU SAD IT'S NOT ACTUALLY GOLD?

681 — England's first recorded boxing match is a real knockout. The Second Duke of Albemarle, Christopher Monck, organized the bout between his butler and his butcher. There were no gloves, barely any safety rules, and the butcher made mincemeat out of the butler.

1863 — **James Plimpton patents four-wheeled "rocker skates,"** which are like the ones we know today that can be steered leaning to the right or left. They're a huge success, although roller-skating birthday parties take another few decades to catch on.

1912 — Geophysicist and meteorologist Alfred Wegener presents his theory of continental drift. The idea is that all seven continents on the globe were once one supercontinent (Wegener called it Pangaea), which gradually broke apart because of the movement of the earth's crust. Come back, Africa—North America misses you!

2021 — Supporters of Donald Trump attack the U.S. Capitol building to try to stop Congress from verifying Joe Biden's victory in the 2020 presidential election. It is the first attempt in American history to prevent a peaceful transfer of power.

JANUARY 7

785 — Jean-Pierre Blanchard and John Jefferies cross the English Channel from England to France, becoming the first people to travel between two countries via hot-air balloon. It was not exactly a pleasant journey. Along the way, the balloon started falling, and they had to start throwing things overboard to lighten the load—including Blanchard's pants!

789 — Members of the first Electoral College are appointed under the new U.S. Constitution. A month later, on February 4, this group elects George Washington as America's first president. (Side note: Do you think instead of using a mirror, George Washington just looked at a dollar bill?)

990 — **The Leaning Tower of Pisa is closed** because it's leaning too much and about to topple over. Over the years, engineers have worked to straighten the tower—but not too much. Would you want to take a trip to see the Totally Straight Tower of Pisa?

the UH-OH ANGLE

JANUARY 8

1800 A child who will eventually become known as the Wild Boy of Aveyron walks out of the woods in southern France and is taken into care. No one knew what had happened to his original family, but Victor, as he was named, had lived most of his life in the wild. After being taken in by kind people, he struggled with language and the rules of society. He hated wearing clothes, liked to crawl around on all fours, and was totally comfortable sleeping outside—even in the snow!

2014 **The first known interstellar meteor hits earth**, plopping to the bottom of the ocean off the coast of Papua New Guinea. Interstellar means that it traveled from another solar system. That's quite a long trip, almost as long as the meteor's name: CNEOS 2014-01-08.

JANUARY 9

1768 **Philip Astley, who mastered the ability to ride a horse while standing on its back, reopens his famed equestrian show**, now recognized as the world's first modern circus, at a new indoor venue in London. Astley's circus evolved to include music; domesticated animals; death-defying acrobats; and even *more* terrifying, clowns.

2007 Apple Inc. CEO Steve Jobs announces the first iPhone. He describes it as "an iPod, a phone, and Internet communicator." If you are wondering what an iPod is, ask an old person (you know, someone older than 15).

2009 The first Bitcoin ever created—known as the genesis block—is mined. The creator, who goes by the pseudonym Satoshi Nakamoto, mined up to 1.1 million Bitcoins, which were worth a whopping zero dollars back then. But today? If Satoshi had held on to those coins, at the time this book was printed, that stash would be worth about $29 billion. No wonder Satoshi doesn't want anyone to know who they are —everyone would constantly be asking for a loan!

What Is the U.N.?

The U.N. is an international organization of 193 member states whose goal is to foster peace throughout the world, provide aid to those in need, and protect human rights and the environment. Prior to the U.N., an organization called the League of Nations was formed. When the league failed to prevent the outbreak of WWII, the U.N. took over its mission. Since then, U.N. peacekeeping forces have helped end conflicts in many nations, including Cambodia, El Salvador, Guatemala, and Namibia.

1901 • Oil! A drilling derrick in Texas sends an enormous gusher of crude oil into the air, sparking a boom that will help transform powered transportation—while also making a big ol' mess.

1946 • **The first session of the General Assembly of the United Nations (U.N.) is called to order**, attended by representatives of 51 nations.

1985 • British inventor Clive Sinclair rolls out the Sinclair C5, a battery-powered three-wheeled vehicle. It didn't exactly take off (it reached a top speed of 15 mph), but it did pave the way for the future battery-powered car industry. (Think of it as Tesla's grandpa.)

JANUARY 11

1896 • **British doctor John Hall-Edwards is the first person to use X-rays for a medical exam.** In this case, the patient is a colleague who volunteers to have a needle jammed in their hand to demonstrate how X-rays can "see" it. (Yelling "Ouch!" is a perfectly healthy reaction to reading that last sentence.) Oh, by the way, X-rays are called that because the scientist who discovered them, Wilhelm Röntgen, didn't know what they were or how they behaved. "X" was supposed to be a temporary name, but it just stuck. Kind of like that needle.

1922 • Insulin is used for the first time to treat diabetes, saving the life of its first patient, a 14-year-old boy from Canada. Symptoms of diabetes were recorded as far back as ancient Egypt in manuscripts written in 1500 BCE.

1964 • Surgeon General Luther L. Terry, M.D., releases the first report to officially show how terrible smoking is for people's health. Before that, unbelievably, lots of people—including some doctors!—said that smoking was actually good for you.

X-RAY-O-MATIC

JANUARY 12

...HELLO?

1967 — **Dr. James Bedford is the first person to be treated with cryonics**, which means he was put in a deep freeze shortly after dying with the hope that he'd be thawed out in the future when new medicine could save him. (And hopefully, cure his epic case of brain freeze.)

1995 — Thirty-one gray wolves are reintroduced into Yellowstone National Park, successfully reviving the wolf population after they vanished due to excessive hunting. The National Park Service is constantly monitoring populations of animals, making sure that there is a balance of life and resources for all the animals that call these parks home.

2010 — A devastating 7.0 earthquake rocks Haiti, killing an estimated 300,000 people and leaving more than 1 million homeless. The horrible event leads to a global rescue and recovery effort.

JANUARY 13

2008 — Adventurers **James Castrission and Justin Jones paddle in a kayak all the way from Australia to New Zealand**—more than 2,060 miles!—over the course of 62 days. Did they miss the ferry? The adventurous duo has accomplished all types of feats, such as walking across the largest blackwater swamp in North America. They slept in hammocks to stay above the water (not to mention the snakes and alligators).

JANUARY 14

1784 — The signing of the Treaty of Paris officially ends the American War for Independence. George Washington did not chant, "U-S-A! U-S-A!" in the face of any British person he could find, but he should have.

2005 — **The European Space Agency's probe _Huygens_ parachutes onto the surface of Titan, Saturn's largest moon.** It's the first lunar landing in the outer solar system. And probably the first time a space probe said, "Weeee!"

★ It's World Religion Day!

This day is designed to bring harmony by recognizing and honoring all the different religions practiced by people around the world. There are thousands of different religions, and here are some significant holidays celebrated by five major faith groups.

1 BUDDHISM
Wesak, honors the Buddha's birth, enlightenment, and death.

2 CHRISTIANITY
Christmas, celebrates the birth of Jesus Christ.

3 HINDU
Diwali, a festival of lights, paying respect to the triumph of good over evil.

4 ISLAM
Ramadan, the ninth month of the Muslim calendar, observed by fasting from sunrise to sunset.

5 JUDAISM
Yom Kippur, a day of atonement.

1967 The National Football League Green Bay Packers trounce the American Football League Kansas City Chiefs, 35-10, in the first AFL–NFL World Championship, which was later redubbed as Super Bowl I. Wonder if the commercials were any good back then?

2001 Wikipedia, the free online encyclopedia written and edited by volunteers, is launched into operation by Jimmy Wales and Larry Sanger. At least that's what it says on Wikipedia.

2009 In an event called **the Miracle on the Hudson**, US Airways Airbus A320 suffers catastrophic engine damage after it flies into a flock of geese just after takeoff. With no time to spare and no chance to get back to the airport, pilot Chesley "Sully" Sullenberger crash-lands the plane in the Hudson River in New York City. Despite the impact and the frigid waters, all passengers and crew members survived, and Sully became a national hero.

WE MADE IT!

JANUARY 16

1547 • Teenager Ivan IV is crowned first czar of Russia. He sure earned his nickname Ivan the Terrible, with fits of rage that resulted in the death of family members. He was extremely paranoid and formed a police force called the *oprichnina* that dressed all in black and rode black horses to spread fear and intimidation among his subjects and those he thought were his enemies.

What Is a Czar?

Czar (pronounced "zar") is a Russian word that means ruler or emperor. They had total and complete power. That is, until they got overthrown. The last czar of Russia was Czar Nicholas II, who ruled from 1894 until he was forced to abdicate (meaning, give up his throne) in 1917.

2006 • Nicknamed Africa's Iron Lady, **Ellen Johnson Sirleaf is sworn in as president of Liberia**, the first elected woman head of an African country. In 2011, she was awarded the Nobel Peace Prize for her efforts to promote peace and advocate for women's rights.

JANUARY 17

1921 • **P.T. Selbit is the first magician to perform the "sawing a person in half" trick.** His assistant, Betty Barker, stepped out of the box in one piece and took a bow at the end of the performance—phew!

1977 • Japanese author Tarō Gomi writes and draws the kid classic *Everyone Poops*. We'll give you 10 bucks if you can say that aloud without giggling.

1991 • U.S. military operations in the First Gulf War begin with Operation Desert Storm, the bombing attack on Iraq after Iraqi troops invaded nearby Kuwait.

1997 • Norwegian explorer Børge Ousland completes the first solo expedition across Antarctica on foot. The icy journey on cross-country skis covered 1,764 miles, took 64 days, and was billed as unsupported, which means he carried everything he needed. Think of that next time you feel like your backpack is too heavy to lug all the way to math class.

1593 — It's Royal Thai Armed Forces Day (Wan Kong Thap Thai). The day commemorates King Naresuan of Siam's victory against Crown Prince Mingyi Swa in an elephant duel. (Note: That means that they fought while riding elephants, *not* that they threw elephants at each other.)

1911 — A Curtiss biplane is the first airplane to land on a ship. Eugene Ely piloted the plane and touched down safely on a platform attached to the deck of the USS *Pennsylvania* cruiser. Aircraft carriers—basically a moveable landing strip—quickly became the centerpiece of America's naval force, allowing pilots to fly missions anywhere in the world.

1943 — **Sliced bread is temporarily banned in the U.S.** No, not because government officials hated peanut butter and jelly sandwiches, but because they thought it would help reduce demand for equipment that the government needed while fighting World War II.

JANUARY 19

It's National Popcorn Day!

WHO INVENTED POPCORN?

First, it is important to know that the kind of corn that pops is different from the kind we eat on the cob. Corn for popping is called *zea mays everta*, and some of the oldest known popcorn cobs were found in a cave in New Mexico in 1948. Scientific analysis determined that they were more than 5,000 years old! The good news is that popcorn that old won't get stuck in your teeth; the bad news is that it will probably break them. Not a good snack.

1883 — Things start buzzing in Roselle, New Jersey, as Thomas Edison flicks on the first electric lighting system with overhead wires. Here in the U.S., it is easy to take for granted that we can charge a phone whenever we want, but around the world, there are still hundreds of millions of people without easy access to electricity.

1809 — Poet and author Edgar Allan Poe is born in Boston. Famous for super creepy works like the epic poem *The Raven* and the short story "The Tell-Tale Heart," he is also considered the father of the detective story. If you ever need to stay up late, forget caffeine, just read one of his spooky tales. You won't sleep a wink.

JANUARY 20

1981 Just hours after Ronald Reagan's presidential inauguration, **52 Americans who had been taken hostage at the U.S. embassy in Tehran, Iran, are released after spending 444 days in captivity.** Their captors were radical students who supported Iran's supreme leader, the anti-American cleric Ayatollah Ruhollah Khomeini.

2021 **Kamala Harris is sworn in as vice president,** making her the first female, first Black woman, and first Asian American person to hold the office of the VP in the United States.

JANUARY 21

1793 The French Revolution, led by citizens who are disgusted with their poor living conditions and the ruinous economic ways of the country's monarchy and aristocracy, gets bloody as King Louis XVI loses his head (and life) by guillotine. Louis's famous wife, Marie Antoinette, also met her death by guillotine as the revolution took a turn into a violent period known as the Reign of Terror.

1976 **Airliner Concorde starts flying passengers between New York and London on planes that travel twice the speed of sound.** On a normal commercial jet, that trip takes about eight hours. In 1996, the Concorde set the record at two hours, 52 minutes, and 59 seconds. By the time you asked the flight attendant for some extra ice in your soda, you were on the ground.

2017 Millions of people throughout the United States and the world take part in the Women's March. The march was a rallying cry for the importance of gender equality and civil rights. Researchers say it is the largest single-day protest in U.S. history.

What Happens When You Break the Speed of Sound?

Sound travels in waves that move at 770 mph in warm air at sea level. That's fast, but if you can go faster than that, sound has to catch up to you. So, for example, if you were on a boat when the Concorde flew over at top speed, it might seem like it is silent. But once the sound caught up—boom! Literally. The sound waves that radiate to the ground are called a sonic boom, and if you can hear it, that means you are standing in the boom carpet (don't worry about taking off your shoes, boom carpets can't get dirty).

JANUARY 22

1506
On this day, Switzerland sends 150 elite fighters to protect the life of Pope Julius II at the Vatican. And they never leave. The Swiss Guards, who dress in brightly colored uniforms, still stand watch at the Vatican today as the Pope's personal army of bodyguards.

1869
Grigori Yefimovich Rasputin is born. Once adult, Rasputin claimed to have mystical powers and fooled Czar Nicholas II and high-ranking leaders into believing he could heal the sick and control the destiny of the entire nation. They all believed him...until they didn't. He was eventually labeled a fraud and, due to his outrageous behavior, was poisoned, shot, and tossed into an ice-covered river. Er, happy birthday?

1997
While walking through a park in Tulsa, **Lottie Williams gets hit (harmlessly) on the shoulder by a piece of metal. An investigation determines that it is actually a piece of a disintegrated rocket**, making Lottie the only known person on earth to be hit by space debris. Just call her Lucky Lottie!

JANUARY 23

1368
After being under the rule of the Mongols, China returns to self-governance with the start of the Ming dynasty. Everyone must have liked the Ming dynasty a lot because it lasted nearly 300 years.

1960
Challenger Deep is the deepest point in the earth's oceans, about seven miles straight down. And on this day, U.S. Navy Lieutenant Don Walsh and Swiss scientist Jacques Piccard climbed into research submarine *Trieste* and took a five-hour, 35,800-foot descent to touch bottom. Wow, they sure could hold their breath for a long time, huh?

1978
Sweden is the first nation to ban aerosols that contain harmful chlorofluorocarbons (CFCs), which damage the ozone layer and contribute to climate change. Nearly every country on earth has since followed Sweden's lead.

2020
Using a 3D print of an ancient Egyptian mummy's vocal cords, British scientists make it possible to hear the mummy's voice. After dying in the desert 3,000 years ago, we're guessing it asked for a glass of water.

I LOVE MY MUMMY

1848 • While building a sawmill on the American River near Colma, California, James W. Marshall finds gold on the riverbed. Word gets out, and the **California Gold Rush begins**, the largest migration of people yet in U.S. history. People who moved out to California in 1849 were known as the forty-niners, which is how San Francisco's NFL got its name. California wasn't the first gold rush in America, however. Fifty years earlier, a 17-pound gold nugget was discovered in North Carolina. And an estimated 30,000 people moved there in search of gold...and a store that sold shovels.

1972 • Twenty-eight years after World War II ends, hunters in the jungle of Guam make a startling discovery. They find Shoichi Yokoi, a Japanese army sergeant who doesn't know the war is over and is hiding, waiting for orders from his commanders. He was returned to Japan as a hero and admired for his ability to survive on the natural resources that surrounded him, including breakfasts of eels and rats.

JANUARY 25

Four Frozen Facts About Antarctica

1 Antarctica holds most of the world's fresh water locked in its ice sheet.

2 So little precipitation falls that Antarctica is technically a desert.

3 The South Pole gets six months of constant daylight during its summer and six months of constant darkness during its winter.

4 If you are standing at the south pole, every direction you face is north.

1840 • A long time ago, no one really knew what was at the bottom-most part of the globe. Was there just ice? A bunch of whales? Nothing? Then American naval officer Charles Wilkes and his crew took a voyage on the USS *Vincennes* to find out for sure and pulled their ship up to an unknown continent that was named Antarctica.

1921 • Czech writer Karel Čapek pens a futuristic play called R.U.R. (*Rossum's Universal Robots*), which contains the first known use of the word robot. Consider it C-3PO's weird old uncle.

JANUARY 26

1788 • Captain Arthur Phillip guides a fleet of 11 British ships carrying 700 convicted criminals to colonize Australia as a country. The journey takes eight months, and the date they finally land at Sydney becomes known as Australia Day. The anniversary is controversial, and many refer to it as Invasion Day, as the new colonists brought oppression to the First Nations people who were already there.

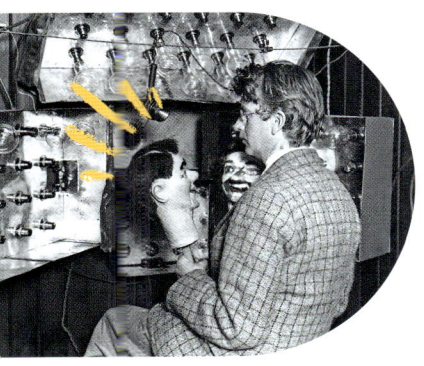

1875 • The first electric dental drill is patented by George Green. Hey, George? Next time keep your big ideas to yourself!

1924 • Go, Chuck, go! U.S. speed skater Charles Jewtraw is the first athlete to win a gold medal in the first Winter Olympics.

1926 • **Scottish inventor John Logie Baird gives the first demonstration of a working TV.** The audience was treated to a show featuring two ventriloquist dummies, which makes you wonder how long it took the first person in history to say, "Change the channel!"

JANUARY 27

1756 • Wolfang Amadeus Mozart is born. The genius composer wrote more than 800 pieces of music.

1945 • With the end of World War II, **Soviet troops enter the concentration camp Auschwitz, liberating the survivors** inside its barbed-wired walls and revealing the horrors of the Holocaust to the world. The Nazis, led by Adolph Hitler, believed that they could rule the world as a "master race" by destroying all those of Jewish descent and other groups. About 1.1 million people were murdered at Auschwitz alone, and over the course of the Holocaust, 6 million Jews and 5 million others (including prisoners of war, people with other ethnic backgrounds, Roma, disabled people, and gay people) perished due to Hitler's evil plan. It is estimated that a total of 40 to 50 million people died over the course of WWII.

Never Forget

In 2005, the United Nations General Assembly declared January 27 as International Holocaust Remembrance Day. Across the globe, nations hold ceremonies to honor the millions who died as well as the survivors who lived through one of the most terrible events in human history.

JANUARY 28

1896 — Crazed automobile driver **Walter Arnold is given the world's first speeding ticket** for driving through town at four times the speed limit. That's right, he was going 8 mph in a 2-mph zone! The punishment for his lead-foot ways? One shilling, which is equivalent to about 6 cents. That'll teach him, right?

1958 — It's International LEGO Day, which celebrates when Ole Kirk Christiansen filed the original patent for LEGO bricks.

1986 — The space shuttle *Challenger* lifts off from Cape Canaveral, Florida, with high school teacher Christa McAuliffe on board. She had won a competition to become the first teacher to journey into space. Tragically, shortly after takeoff, the *Challenger* exploded, killing all seven people on board.

2017 — Serena Williams wins her 23rd Grand Slam title, the most won by any player, male or female, in tennis's Open era. Her opponent? Her big sister Venus. (Can you say "awkward"?) Serena retired from tennis in 2022, and her record has yet to be broken.

❓ Did You Know?

The LEGO factory never stops working. If you made a line with all the bricks sold every year, they would reach around the world more than five times!

JANUARY 29

1595 — It is believed that William Shakespeare's play ***Romeo and Juliet* is first performed** on this day, while it took another two years to be officially published. Shakespeare, known as the Bard, is considered the greatest English-speaking writer in history...by those who believe he actually wrote the more than 36 plays and 150 sonnets he gets credit for. Over the years, scholars and famous people like Henry James, Mark Twain, and Charlie Chaplin have publicly doubted that Shakespeare really penned all these great works. But there has been no definitive proof that he didn't, so all the haters can shuteth up, as the Bard might write.

2018 — *Black Panther* premieres: It's the first Marvel Cinematic Universe film that has a Black director and a mostly Black cast. And it is awesome. Wakanda forever!

RUSH HOUR

1826 — **The world's first major suspension bridge opens** between an island and the mainland of Wales, allowing livestock traders to move their cattle faster. Hey, buddy, *moooove* along!

1882 — Franklin D. Roosevelt—America's 32nd president—is born. He was routinely named one of the country's greatest presidents, as he led America through the Great Depression and World War II with powerful actions and inspiring words like, "The only thing we have to fear is fear itself." He served a record four terms as president, and it is a record that will likely never be beaten after the 22nd Amendment of the U.S. Constitution officially limited presidents to two full terms (plus up to two years of a predecessor's term if they die in office.)

1933 — **The Lone Ranger**, one of the most famous fictional characters, has his first adventure told on radio station WXYZ in Detroit.

1996 — NBA superstar Earvin "Magic" Johnson announces his return to the game after retiring four years earlier when he contracted the virus that causes AIDS. Since then, Magic has continued to tirelessly advocate for research and support for those affected by HIV.

JANUARY 31

!yaD drawkcaB lanoitaN s'tI

(It's National Backward Day!)

1865 — Congress votes to pass the 13th Amendment, which will abolish slavery in every state in America by December 18 that same year.

1990 — The first McDonald's opens in Moscow. Citizens of the Soviet Union go nuts, standing in huge lines to spend several days' worth of pay on Big Macs and fries.

THIS DAY IN *my* HISTORY
JANUARY

Fill in any memorable events from your life here.

1 ....

2 ....

3 ....

4 ....

5 ....

6 ....

7 ....

8 ....

9 ....

10 ....

11 ....

12 ....

13 ....

14 ....

15 ....

16 ....

17 ....

18 ....

19 ....

20 ....

21 ....

22 ....

23 ....

24 ....

25 ....

26 ....

27 ....

28 ....

29 ....

30 ....

31 ....

FEBRUARY 1

T'S BLACK HISTORY MONTH! First celebrated as National Negro Week in February of 1926, the tribute became a month-long event starting in 1970. It celebrates the great achievements of all Black people in America in science, the arts, and business. The month was chosen because Abraham Lincoln and **abolitionist Frederick Douglass** were both born in February.

2009 ● Iceland's prime minister, Johanna Sigurdardottir, becomes the first national head of a government who is proudly and openly part of the LGBTQ+ community.

UNAR NEW YEAR. The exact day for this holiday changes every year, as it is timed to the lunar cycle, but the thing that does stay the same? It's always one big party! Lunar New Year has been celebrated for thousands of years to honor ancestors and welcome good luck. Traditional celebrations include dressing and decorating in the color red and setting off tons of fireworks. This is because of the legend of the monster Nian, who was part lion and part bull and attacked villagers on the first day of every year—but it feared loud noises *and* the color red. So, the tradition began to start the year off with a bang!

❓ Did You Know?

The Lunar zodiac assigns an animal sign to each new year. Look for the year you were born to find your animal sign.

If the new year falls under the same sign as yours—congrats, you're going to have amazingly good luck for an entire year!

FEBRUARY 2

1709 — Meet the real-life Robinson Crusoe: Scottish naval officer Alexander Selkirk is marooned on a deserted island in the Pacific for four years and four months before being rescued. Luckily, the island was full of animals and plants for him to live on. Unluckily, well, like we just said, he was stuck there for four years and four months.

1887 — **The first Groundhog Day celebration is held,** featuring a rodent today known as Punxsutawney Phil. If Phil comes out of his hole and sees his shadow, he gets scared and runs back inside, predicting six more weeks of winter weather. No shadow means an early spring. Wait...a sunny day means more bad weather? Phil, we know you're basically just a big rat, but that doesn't make any sense.

2015 — Seventeen-year-old New Zealand golfer Lydia Ko becomes the youngest to be ranked number one in the world. Some advice? Do not challenge her to a game of mini golf.

FEBRUARY 3

What Was the Space Race?

Do you know someone you always find yourself competing with in running races or Ping-Pong tournaments or seeing who can hold their breath the longest? That was basically the United States and the Soviet Union between the 1950s and 1970s—and they were battling to see who could dominate space exploration. But in the late 1970s, scientists shifted from trying to outdo each other to working together. Since 1998, astronauts and cosmonauts have shared flights to the International Space Station.

1870 — The 15th Amendment to the U.S. Constitution is ratified and guarantees all Black American men the right to vote.

1916 — While it is up for debate, some music scholars credit the Versatile Four quartet with making the first recording of jazz music with the song "Down Home Rag" by Wilbur Sweatman.

1966 — Soviet Union's *Luna 9* **is the first spacecraft to touch down on the surface of the moon and remain in one piece.** Why wasn't there a famous speech made? Because no one was on board.

1995 — Eileen Collins becomes the first female space shuttle pilot.

2005 — Alberto Gonzales is confirmed by the Senate as the nation's first Hispanic Attorney General, the top legal officer in the country. Attorneys General advise the president and act as the people's lawyer for U.S. citizens.

FEBRUARY 4

💡 Did You Know?

Babby, Crabby, Deafy, Flabby, Gaspy, Hotsy, Lazy, Nifty, Shifty, Thrifty, and Weezy were some of the other names considered for the seven dwarfs. What on earth would a Hotsy dwarf be like?

WEEZY   SHIFTY   CRABBY

1938 • **Disney releases _Snow White and the Seven Dwarfs_**, the first feature-length animated film in theaters nationwide.

2004 • Mark Zuckerberg launches the original Facebook, which he created in his Harvard dorm room. Although there has been a decline in users who aren't 40-year-old moms and dads, at last count, there were still 2.96 billion Facebook users around the world. In some countries, Facebook is basically the Internet, which is why making sure misinformation is controlled on social media platforms is so vital.

In October of 2021, Zuckerberg announced that his company Facebook was being renamed Meta, prompting everyone in the world to ask the same question: "What the heck is the metaverse?"

FEBRUARY 5

1869 • Two miners in Australia find the world's largest gold nugget. Named the Welcome Stranger, it weighed 167 pounds and was found stuck in the roots of a tree. (If we were you, we'd put this book down and go try to dig up some trees!)

1953 • **Candy rationing is finally over in the U.K.** 11 years after the end of World War II. After 11 years, that first piece of chocolate must have tasted pretty darn sweet.

What Was Rationing?

During World War II, the governments of the U.S. and the U.K. asked their citizens to cut back on using and eating certain things so that the supplies (and the labor it took to make them) could be concentrated on the war effort. Sugar, gasoline, cars, meat, and shoes were just some of the things ordinary citizens didn't use as much.

VICTORY
NEVER TASTED SO SWEET.

FEBRUARY 6

1921   Already famous for short comedy films, **Charlie Chaplin releases his directorial debut, *The Kid*, a full-length silent film.** It was an instant hit, and trust us on this, even though it was made more than 100 years ago and has no sound, it is hilarious.

2018   For the first launch of SpaceX's *Falcon Heavy* rocket, company head Elon Musk packs in a surprise: The rocket's test payload is his Tesla Roadster with a mannequin named Starman behind the steering wheel. The Roadster and Starman are released and are still in an orbit that takes them on a loop around Mars and the sun. Eventually, scientists say, the car may be drawn in and smack into either the earth or Venus. But you don't need to keep looking up—it won't happen for tens of millions of years.

FEBRUARY 7

1959   Two pilots from Las Vegas, Robert Timm and John Cook, set the flight-endurance record by flying for 64 days, 22 hours, and 19 minutes without stopping. Twice a day, the pilots would steer their plane just 20 feet over a closed roadway, where it would snag a gas hose from a speeding truck and refuel. The process lasted three minutes, and the plane would launch back up. To fend off any accusations of cheating (such as sneaking in landings in the middle of the night), a chase car painted the plane's tires bright white soon after takeoff. The idea was that if they landed, the white paint would get dirty and give them away.

1964   An airplane lands at New York's Kennedy Airport—and brings Beatlemania with it. The Beatles were a rock and roll group that eventually had a record-breaking 20 number one hit albums. Everywhere the Beatles went, screaming fans followed. At one concert, the Beatles had to stop playing because the fans were screaming so loud that the band couldn't hear their own music.

1984   **Astronaut Bruce McCandless performs the first untethered spacewalk.** (Meaning, he had nothing keeping him tied to space shuttle *Challenger*.) McCandless relied on his backpack-like Manned Maneuvering Unit (MMU) to prevent him from drifting off into the depths of outer space. That is one brave guy!

2021   The Tampa Bay Buccaneers beat the Kansas City Chiefs in the Super Bowl—the first time in history a team wins the big game in its home stadium. We're sure Chiefs fans are thrilled to learn this fact.

1672 — **Isaac Newton presents a famous scientific paper explaining how he used a prism to show that sunlight** (thought to be pure white) is actually made up of a rainbow of seven colors: red, orange, yellow, green, blue, indigo, and violet. The supersmart scientists who read Newton's paper did not exclaim, "So pretty!" but they should have.

ROY G BIV

1865 — Austrian monk and scientist Gregor Mendel presents his research paper "Experiments in Plant Hybridization," which uses his study of pea plants to explain the concept of dominant and recessive genes. Mendel is known as the father of modern genetics. Who knew pea plants could be so interesting?

1910 — **The Boy Scouts of America is founded** by William D. Boyce, with the purpose of teaching kids the value of teamwork, leadership, and moral strength. (And also, how to tie really complicated knots.) In 2018, the BSA opened their program to allow girls to join in on the campfire fun.

1986 — Big heroes come in all sizes. NBA superstar Spud Webb walks onto the court during 1986's NBA All-Star Weekend and claims the Slam Dunk Contest champion crown. What's so special about that? Standing just 5'7", Webb was one of the shortest professional ballers in NBA history. With amazing ups and rim-shaking two-handed throwdowns, he beat his Atlanta Hawks teammate Dominique Wilkins, who was 6'8"—more than a foot taller than Webb! He might not have had long arms and legs, but Webb had a long career, dazzling crowds and defying expectations for 12 seasons in the NBA.

FEBRUARY 9

1876 • Sardines are canned in the United States for the first time by Julius Wolff in Eastport, Maine. "Why?" asks anyone who ever opened and smelled a can of sardines. OK, the reason is that canning keeps fish edible for a long time and makes it easily shippable over great distances. But still, pretty gross.

1969 • First flight of a wide-body jumbo jet, the 747. The new, massive airplane style meant more passengers, more comfort—and, well, more barf bags.

1971 • Pitcher Leroy "Satchel" Paige is the first player to be nominated and then inducted into the Baseball Hall of Fame based on his record in the Negro League. The fastball-throwing machine's incredible career bridged five decades (the average Major League Baseball career lasts two to five years), and legendary Yankee Joe DiMaggio once said Paige was "the best and fastest pitcher I've ever faced."

★ **It's National Pizza Day!**

Hundreds of years ago, the hardworking but poor people of the Italian city of Naples needed food that was cheap, fast to make, and easy to eat. Thus, the ooey-gooey saucy delight was born. What do you think is the best pizza topping? (If you said anchovies, you're wrong.)

FEBRUARY 10

1722 • The infamous pirate Black Bart is killed in a cannonball battle. He and his busy crew of bad guys plundered about 400 ships before their reign of high-seas terror ended. While we may think of pirates as people from a long time ago, they still operate today, especially off the coasts of Southeast Asia and Africa.

1996 • **World chess champion Garry Kasparov loses the first game of a six-game match against Deep Blue, an IBM computer.** Even though Deep Blue could evaluate 200 million moves in a second, Kasparov eventually won the match. We hope Deep Blue wasn't a sore loser.

What Is the Spanish Flu?

The Spanish flu wasn't called that because it originated in Spain. The pandemic occurred during World War I, and countries involved in the fight suppressed news about the outbreak because they didn't want it to bring down the morale of their armies. But because Spain was neutral during WWI, Spanish newspapers reported on all its horrible details. And because Spanish news sources were one of the only places people could read about it, a misunderstanding grew that the country was ground zero for the worldwide outbreak. It is now referred to as the 1918 influenza pandemic.

1918 The 1918 influenza pandemic begins spreading throughout the world. One of the deadliest pandemics in history, it infected 500 million people (that's nearly one-third of everyone on earth) and killed at least 50 million. In comparison, by the beginning of 2023, the COVID-19 pandemic had killed about 6.6 million.

1990 **Freedom activist Nelson Mandela is released after being imprisoned for 27 years in South Africa.** Mandela tirelessly fought to end apartheid in South Africa, which was a legal system that said people of different races could not live together and forced most Black people to live far outside the city in poverty-stricken developments. His actions got him arrested, but he kept fighting and inspiring others, even after he was jailed. In 1994, Mandela was elected the first Black president of South Africa in a fully multiracial election.

FEBRUARY 12

1909 The National Association for the Advancement of Colored People (the NAACP) is founded, dedicated to fighting for equality and social justice in America.

1912 Today is the day that Emperor Puyi was forced to give up his throne, making him the last emperor of China. But don't worry, he had plenty of time to find a new job. Puyi was only 6 years old at the time.

1994 **Norway's most famous painting, *The Scream* by Edvard Munch, is stolen from a museum** by two thieves who leave a note on the blank wall reading, "Thousand thanks for the bad security!" The note should have said, "See you in three months!" because that's when the thieves were caught, and the painting was recovered.

FEBRUARY 13

1866 ● **Possibly the very first bank robbery is carried out by Jesse James.** The outlaw eluded law enforcement for 15 years while he and his gang robbed banks, stagecoaches, trains, and basically anyplace you might find lots of money.

1945 ● Toward the end of World War II, an Allied firebombing raid utterly destroys the German city of Dresden. More than 3,400 tons of explosives were dropped by 1,200 British and American planes, reducing the once-beautiful city to rubble and killing approximately 25,000 people. Many debate whether this amount of destruction was necessary as Germany was already on the verge of surrender.

FEBRUARY 14

270 ● Valentine's Day may have had a not-so-sweet beginning. According to one legend, Roman Emperor Claudius II had trouble enlisting men to join his army and blamed it on their attachment to their wives and children. To solve the problem, he banned all weddings and engagements. A priest named Valentine defied the law and continued to perform marriages anyway. When Claudius heard about this, he had Valentine arrested and beheaded. No wonder he was nicknamed Claudius the Cruel.

1946 ● **ENIAC, the first electric general-purpose computer, is revealed to the public.** Slightly bigger than your laptop, it weighed 30 tons and was made up of 40 nine-foot-tall cabinets.

2016 ● Sophia, one of the first AI-powered humanoid robots, comes to life in the lab at Hanson Robotics. She's been named Innovation Champion for the United Nations Development Programme and has appeared as a guest on TV shows like *The Tonight Show*. Despite what a lot of sci-fi movies have warned, Sophia and her robot friends have not tried to take over the planet and imprison all humans...yet.

1898 A massive explosion sinks the battleship USS *Maine* in Cuba's Havana harbor, triggering the Spanish-American War. When a treaty ended the war in December of the same year, Spain renounced all claims to Cuba, handed Guam and Puerto Rico to the United States, and transferred authority over the Philippines also to the U.S. for $20 million.

1943 **The "We can do it!" poster with Rosie the Riveter debuts** on Westinghouse factory walls during World War II. The poster was made to inspire women to take jobs in defense industries during the war. Prior to this time, most women were discouraged from working, and Rosie became a symbol of female patriotism.

FEBRUARY 16

Who Was King Tut?

King Tut was the pharaoh of Egypt who ruled for 10 years until his death around 1324 BCE. He was just 19 years old when he died, which is why he is referred to as the Boy King. Tut was found with a hole in his skull, which made people wonder if he had been murdered. But further research revealed that the hole was made during the mummification process. His sealed burial chambers were filled with amazing treasures and artifacts that have been exhibited around the world.

1923 In the Valley of Kings in Egypt, **English archaeologist Howard Carter steps inside the long-sealed burial chamber of the ancient Egyptian ruler King Tutankhamen, known as King Tut.** Among the remarkable objects he and Egyptian workers found were three coffins nestled inside each other, with the final one being made of solid gold and containing Tut's mummy.

1933 Astronomer Fritz Zwicky theorizes that there is an invisible material called dark matter that prevents spinning galaxies from flying apart. "That's nonsense," said his doubters, who went back to wondering what kind of cheese the moon was made of.

FEBRUARY 17

Surprise someone with an unexpected compliment, hold a door open, or actually look up from your phone when your parents ask you how school was today. They'll cry tears of joy!

BEEP! BEEP!

1869 • Russian chemist Dmitri Mendeleev is the first person to write down the periodic table of the elements. Luckily for students cramming for chemistry tests back then, there were only 63 known elements at the time as opposed to the 118 we know today.

1972 • Move over Model T, there's a new best-selling car in the world! On this day, **the 15,007,034th Volkswagen Beetle rolls off the assembly line** and into the record books. In 2003, after more than 60 years of production, VW finally slammed the brakes, and the last original Beetle was made.

FEBRUARY 18

1852 • The London Zoo puts in an order for a giant glass "fish house," which will become the world's first public aquarium. More than 300 types of marine species called the Fish House home. (Do London starfish have crumpets and tea at feeding time?)

1885 • Author Mark Twain publishes *The Adventures of Huckleberry Finn* in the U.S. after first publishing it in England. Twain takes an unflinching look at the evils of slavery and tells the thrilling and emotional story of two friends who would do anything to keep each other safe.

1930 • **Elm Farm Ollie is the first cow to fly in an airplane and be milked in the air.** Why? Scientists wanted to see if altitude affected her milk production. *It did not.* The milk they got from Elm Farm Ollie was put into cartons and parachuted down to thirsty people below.

1978 • The first Ironman triathlon takes place in Hawaii and involves competitors swimming 2.4 miles, biking 112 miles, and then running 26.2 miles—a full marathon! We're exhausted just thinking about it.

MILK

FEBRUARY 19

1473 — **Nicolaus Copernicus is born.** A groundbreaking (or sky-breaking) astronomer, Copernicus was the first in the Western scientific tradition to propose that the earth and planets revolved around the sun, rather than the earth being the center of the universe. It wasn't until nearly 200 years later that his theory was widely accepted.

1878 — Very busy inventor Thomas Edison patents the phonograph, one of 1,093 patents he acquired in his lifetime.

1942 — After Pearl Harbor, President Franklin D. Roosevelt signs Executive Order 9066, which forced approximately 120,000 Americans of Japanese ancestry out of their homes to live in prison camps (called internment camps). The government had a mistaken and racist fear that they would commit acts of sabotage. The last Japanese internment camp closed in March 1946, and in 1988 Congress issued a formal apology and awarded $20,000 to more than 80,000 Japanese Americans as reparations for their terrible treatment.

FEBRUARY 20

★ It's National Love Your Pet Day!

But isn't every day Love Your Pet Day? (OK, maybe not the day your dog chewed up your favorite pair of sneakers.)

1986 — The Soviet Union launches the first section (or module) of the Mir space station. Five more modules were added over the next 15 years, allowing 125 cosmonauts and astronauts from 12 countries to live and do research. In 2001, Mir was outdated and directed to descend back into the earth's atmosphere, where it burned up over the Pacific Ocean. (Don't worry, it was remotely controlled!)

FEBRUARY 21

the FIRST STEAM-POWERED LOCOMOTIVE →

1804 — **The first steam-powered locomotive gets chugging and pulls five loaded cars along the tracks in Wales.** No, the locomotive wasn't named Thomas (in fact, it wasn't named anything by its inventor Richard Trevithick), but it was really useful.

1858 — Businessman Edwin T. Holmes installs the world's first electric burglar alarm in Boston. The first thief to try to break in was in for quite a shock.

FEBRUARY 22

1885 — Being that February 22 is George Washington's birthday, this day was officially declared a federal holiday, commonly known as President's Day. But in 1971, President's Day was changed to the third Monday of the month, so people could have more three-day weekends. A present for us all!

1918 — **It's also the birthday of Robert Wadlow,** a guy you wanted nearby if you needed to get something off a shelf. At 8'11", he has been the tallest man in recorded history.

1980 — The Miracle on Ice! If you ever think there is no way you can beat an opponent who is bigger and faster than you, remember this day. The U.S. men's Olympic hockey team, made up of college players, beat the five-time gold-medal-winning Soviet team. The crowd went crazy, and announcer Al Michaels uttered one of the most famous lines in sports broadcasting history: "Do you believe in miracles? Yes!"

8'11"

FEBRUARY 23

1945 • **During the bloody Battle of Iwo Jima in World War II, U.S. Marines raise the American flag on the island's highest peak.** Photographer Joe Rosenthal captured the moment, and it became one of the most famous photos ever taken, winning him the Pulitzer Prize.

2019 • Soccer superstar Lionel Messi scores his 50th hat trick, helping his team, Barcelona, beat Seville 4-2.

What Is a Hat Trick?

A hat trick is typically used to describe when a soccer player or a hockey player scores three points in a single game. Hockey fans typically celebrate a player's hat trick by throwing their hats on the ice. (No, they don't get them back.) But if you want a weirder tradition: Home fans of the Detroit Red Wings hockey team at some point in the season will toss a dead octopus onto the ice for good luck!

FEBRUARY 24

1836 • In San Antonio, Lieutenant Colonel William Travis sends out messages asking for help defending the Alamo, an old Spanish mission and fortress being attacked by the Mexican army. He famously signed off one his messages with "Victory or Death." The Alamo fell to the Mexican army, and many brave fighters were killed, including legendary frontiersman Davy Crockett. The fight inspired Texans to rally with shouts of "Remember the Alamo!" and eventually beat back the Mexican army and make Texas an independent country.

2018 • **The world's biggest art class is held in the Philippines.** Nearly 17,000 students from 200 schools came together and learned how to draw a carnival mask. Snack time must have been quite a feast!

FEBRUARY 25

1862 — The Legal Tender Act is passed by the U.S. Congress, authorizing the government to print paper money (called greenbacks) for people to use instead of silver or gold when making purchases. Can you imagine going to the deli and buying a Gatorade with gold coins?

1870 — Hiram Rhodes Revels becomes the first Black congressman, serving as a senator from Mississippi. Revels fought for the equality of formerly enslaved people and believed that any former members of the Confederacy should be forgiven for their part in the Civil War if they swore loyalty to the United States.

1988 — **Four Jamaicans with very little training compete in the bobsleigh competition at the Olympics.** They didn't win a medal, but they did win the admiration of the viewing public—and of their competitors. There's not a lot of snow and ice in Jamaica (in fact, there's none), so the other Olympic bobsleighers were in awe of these guys who were strong and brave enough to try such a fast-moving and dangerous sport.

FEBRUARY 26

1616 — Italian astronomer Galileo is admonished by the Catholic church for teaching the concept that the earth orbits the sun. It took the church until 1992 to formally apologize for making him recant his scientific discoveries.

1908 — The first commercially produced color movie, *A Visit to the Seaside*, is shown. The eight-minute British short film used a process called Kinemacolor. Before that, film had to be hand-painted frame by frame. Considering that back then there were around 18 frames in just one second, this innovation saved a lot of hand cramping for artists.

1919 — **The Grand Canyon is declared a national park.** How grand is it? A mile deep, 277 miles long, and 18 miles wide. The entire state of Rhode Island could fit inside it!

1935 — RADAR (which stands for Radio Detection and Ranging) is first demonstrated by British scientist Robert Alexander Watson-Watt. It soon came in very handy as way to detect Nazi war planes long before anyone could see them coming.

1827 — Inspired by their travels in Paris, a group of students put on masks and costumes and dance through the streets of New Orleans—the city's first Mardi Gras parade. New Orleans's Mardi Gras is basically the world's biggest party that goes on for weeks and weeks. It has been canceled only 14 times in its nearly 200-year history.

1998 — The most expensive slice of wedding cake is sold for $29,900 at Sotheby's auction. The cake was baked in 1937 for the Duke and Duchess of Windsor. Proceeds from the sale were given to charity, and hopefully the slice was given to a garbage can. Would you want to bite into a 61-year-old slice of cake?

FEBRUARY 28

1953 — **Scientists James D. Watson and Francis H.C. Crick announce that they have determined the double-helix structure of DNA.** While people knew that genetics were passed down from one generation to the next, no one knew how exactly. After making their discovery, Crick supposedly marched into a nearby pub and announced they "had found the secret of life." Knowledge of DNA has helped in many fields, from developing medical treatment to identifying or exonerating criminals.

1991 — The Gulf War officially ends as U.S.-led coalition forces push the invading Iraqi army out of Kuwait.

FEBRUARY 29

★ **It's Leap Day!**

Every four years, February gets an extra day. That's because while the calendar says a year is 365 days long, it actually takes earth about 365.25 days to revolve around the sun. That might seem like a tiny difference, but over the years it adds up and can put our planet totally out of whack with our calendars. Adding in an extra day keeps everything synced, which is good news for accuracy but bad news if you were born on this day and have a birthday only once every four years.

THIS DAY IN *my* HISTORY
FEBRUARY

Fill in any memorable events from your life here.

1 ....

2 ....

3 ....

4 ....

5 ....

6 ....

7 ....

8 ....

9 ....

10 ....

11 ....

12 ....

13 ....

14 ....

15 ....

16 ....

17 ....

18 ....

19 ....

20 ....

21 ....

22 ....

23 ....

24 ....

25 ....

26 ....

27 ....

28 ....

29 ....

IT'S WOMEN'S HISTORY MONTH! First celebrated as Women's History Week in 1980, it has grown into a monthlong celebration in recognition of trailblazing women who have made amazing contributions to American history—from powerful leaders like Susan B. Anthony, who fought for voting rights, to incredible artists like Aretha Franklin, who fought for civil rights and was the first woman inducted into the Rock & Roll Hall of Fame.

1872 — **Yellowstone becomes America's first national park.** It is home to the greatest amount of natural hot springs on earth. A hot spring sounds nice, but do not be tempted to take a dip here—the magma-heated water would boil you alive! Yellowstone has an amazing array of wildlife and famous geysers that periodically erupt, launching boiling water and steam into the air. The National Park System now oversees 424 sites throughout the country. Get some fresh air and see a bear (but don't try to pet one!).

1896 — Scientist Henri Becquerel discovers radioactivity... kind of by accident. He was attempting to do an experiment with sunlight, photographic plates, and uranium salt crystals, but it was a cloudy day, so he threw everything in a drawer. The next day, he saw that the photographic plates had developed from the radiation coming directly from the uranium. This happy accident resulted in him being awarded a Nobel Prize. Did he thank the clouds in his acceptance speech?

1941 — **It's the first appearance of Captain America in a comic book**, and he gets off to a smashing start: The cover features Cap punching Hitler in the face!

★ It's National Pancake Day!

The first known mention of the word pancake is in ancient Greek poems written around 500 BCE. Have you ever written an ode to your favorite breakfast food?

1904

Dr. Seuss is born in Springfield, Massachusetts. And no, his mom didn't name her newborn child Doctor. His real name was Theodor Geisel, and he wrote and drew some of the most famous children's books of all time, like *The Cat in the Hat*, *Green Eggs and Ham*, and *Oh, the Places You'll Go!* Why did he call himself Dr. Seuss? Well, while in college, Theodor got in trouble and was forced to quit his position as editor of the school humor magazine. So he came up with a fake name (Seuss was his mother's maiden name) so that he could continue drawing funny cartoons for the publication. He added the "Dr." part later.

1962

Philadelphia Warriors center Wilt Chamberlain scores 100 points against the New York Knicks, the most points ever by an NBA player in a single game. Chamberlain was 7'11", so it's not hard to imagine why the defense had trouble blocking his shots.

1972

NASA launches the *Pioneer 10* spacecraft, which contains a metal plaque with information about the earth's location and its lifeforms for any extraterrestrials who might see it. NASA lost contact with the spacecraft in 2003 when it was more than 7 billion miles away from earth. Think any aliens have read the plaque yet? What would you have put on it?

★ It's World Teen Mental Wellness Day!

From everyday things like nervous-making school assignments to frightening events happening around the world, we all face a lot of stress that can sometimes feel overwhelming. This day is all about reaching out to friends, family, and trusted adults when you feel sad or depressed *and* knowing that you are not alone.

SUBSTANCE ABUSE AND MENTAL HEALTH SERVICES ADMINISTRATION (SAMHSA) 24-HOUR FREE HELPLINE: 1-800-662-HELP

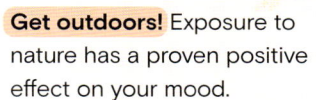

Get outdoors! Exposure to nature has a proven positive effect on your mood.

MARCH 3

1875
On this night at the Victoria Skating Rink in Montreal, Canada, the first recorded indoor hockey game was played. And—no surprise!—it ended in a fight.

1887
A 6-year-old Helen Keller—who lost her sight and hearing after a severe illness when she was a baby—begins learning "touch teaching" techniques from Anne Sullivan. Keller, who many people thought did not have a shot at a normal life, graduated from college and became an international lecturer and activist. Sullivan is remembered by her nickname: the Miracle Worker.

2014
The United Nations declares this to be the first World Wildlife Day to bring attention to the incredible animal and plant life that humans need to protect, like the Chinhai Spiny Newt. It's a cute little amphibian with super pointy ribs that can poke outside of its body to stab anything trying to pick it up or eat it. It's amazing in the wild; terrible at petting zoos.

2017
Nintendo Switch is released. By early 2023, nearly 120 million consoles have been sold. Is one of those millions yours?

DO NOT PET!

MARCH 4

2000
A video-game platform starts selling and just doesn't stop! PlayStation 2 sold 158.7 million units until—game over!—it was discontinued in January 2013. PS2 is one of the best-selling and longest-running consoles in gaming history.

2020
Nik Wallenda is the first person to tightrope walk across an active volcano. He strolled across a wire attached 1,800 feet above the crater floor of the Masaya Volcano in Nicaragua, wearing a mask to avoid breathing the dangerous gasses that could make him dizzy or pass out (neither symptom is very good when standing over an active volcano!).

MARCH 5

1770
The Boston Massacre occurs. British soldiers killed five men in a crowd of colonists who were throwing snowballs, rocks, and sticks at them. Among those killed was Black dock worker and sailor Crispus Attucks, who was the first American killed in the Revolutionary War.

1963
The Hula Hoop is patented by Wham-O company cofounder Arthur "Spud" Melin. It got hips swiveling and cash registers ringing. Historians estimate that 25 million Hula Hoops were sold in its first four months. Wham-O definitely had the magic touch when it came to inventing super fun toys: They also created the Superball, Slip 'N Slide, and the Hacky Sack.

MARCH 6

1475 • **Michelangelo is born.** Considered one of the most famous artists who ever lived, Michelangelo painted, among his many great works, the ceiling of the Sistine Chapel in the Vatican. He also sculpted *David*, a 17-foot-tall marble statue chiseled out of a single piece of marble that had been discarded by other artists who had thought it unusable. Michelangelo is thought to have said, "Every block of stone has a statue inside it, and it is the task of the sculptor to discover it." Think of that next time you are staring at a lump of clay in art class and not sure what to make.

1930 • The first flash-frozen dinners, Birds Eye Frosted Foods, go on sale. Make sure you heat it up—that slice of turkey is not a Popsicle.

MARCH 7

1876 • **Inventor Alexander Graham Bell receives a patent for the telephone.** It allows people to speak to each other from long distances—but bummer, ya can't text yet.

NEW PHONE, WHO'S THIS?

2010 • Kathryn Bigelow becomes the first woman to win an Academy Award for Best Director for her film *The Hurt Locker*.

Here Are Our Nominees for the Most Interesting Facts About the Academy Awards...

1 It is said that they're nicknamed the Oscars because one of the Academy's directors thought that the statue looked like her uncle Oscar.

2 The youngest Oscar winner was 10-year-old Tatum O'Neal, who won Best Supporting Actress for *Paper Moon* in 1974.

3 In 1987, Marlee Matlin became the first deaf performer to win an Oscar.

4 Walt Disney (the guy, not the company) holds the record for the most wins with 26 Oscars. He must have had a huge trophy case.

5 *Shrek* won the first Best Animated Feature award in 2002.

What Is the NYSE?

The NYSE is the largest stock exchange in the world. OK, so what is a stock exchange? It is a system for buying and selling stocks and bonds. A stock is a share in the ownership of a company, and a bond is an agreement to lend money to a company for a certain amount of time. People buy stocks hoping that the company will grow and become more valuable, making their investment worth more. For example, when Chipotle first began trading in 2006, its stock was $22 a share. Seventeen years later, it is valued at around $1,650 per share. So, if your mom bought 100 shares of it back in 2006, her $2,200 investment would have grown to as high as $165,000. That's a lot of burritos! Stocks generally have bigger ups and downs than bonds, which are thought to be steadier and more reliable investments. So you might not make a ton of beans with bonds, but there's less risk of losing them, too.

1817 ● **The New York Stock Exchange (NYSE) is formed.**

1936 ● Speaking of stocks, the first stock car race is held in Daytona Beach, Florida. It was much more thrilling than anyone expected. Twenty-seven cars lined up at the starting line, and only 10 finished. The race was run on the hard-packed sand of the beach; cars got stuck and when the tide started rising, they had to drive through the waves! These days, the Daytona 500 is run on an actual track, which sounds a lot safer but not nearly as fun.

1975 ● The U.N. celebrates the first official International Women's Day, declaring it "a day to recognize the extraordinary acts of women and to stand together, as a united force, to advance gender equality around the world."

MARCH 9

It's National Meatball Day!

From Italy to Thailand to Brazil, many cultures have balls of deliciousness on the menu. No one knows exactly who made the first meatball, but we're glad they did!

1959 ● The first Barbie doll is revealed at the American Toy Fair in New York City. Barbie's inventor was Ruth Handler. After noticing that her daughter stopped playing with her baby dolls and preferred paper dolls of adult women, she created Barbie, the first massproduced American doll with adult features. Billions and billions of Barbie dolls have been sold since, and in 2023, the Barbie movie earned more than $1 billion. People really love this doll!

MARCH 10

1831 • France's King Louis-Philippe I establishes the Foreign Legion fighting force.

1913 • **Ten-pin bowler William Knox rolls the first recorded 300 game in competition.** That means that every single time he stepped up to the line, he threw a strike. (We can't even do that with gutter bumpers.)

What Is the French Foreign Legion?

French law stated that only French citizens could serve in the nation's army. But when they needed more soldiers, the French Foreign Legion was formed, a military force that was originally made up of paid foreign warriors (called mercenaries). Today, the legion is composed of volunteer soldiers who serve in France and abroad.

MARCH 11

1967 • **The U.S. Fish and Wildlife Service publishes its first endangered species list, including the bald eagle**, red wolf, grizzly bear, American alligator, and manatee. Their inclusion puts laws into effect in the U.S. to protect them from hunting and preserve their habitats. The list has worked: Since it was first published, many animals, including the bald eagle, have begun to thrive.

BALD EAGLE

2011 • A massive earthquake on the Pacific Ocean floor creates a tsunami (giant wave) that grows as high as 128 feet tall. It races across the ocean and crashes over Japan's main island of Honshu, killing at least 18,000 people and washing away entire towns. The Fukushima nuclear power plant was destroyed, forcing more than 150,000 to evacuate to escape the harmful leaked radiation. Scientists say it will take up to 40 years to fully clean the area and make it safe for people to return.

2020 • COVID-19 is officially declared a pandemic by the World Health Organization. For something to be considered a pandemic, it needs to be harming a significant number of people in multiple countries and continents.

★ It's National Girl Scout Day!

The first boxes of Girl Scout cookies were sold in 1933 by the organization's Philadelphia Council. Back then, they cost just 23 cents per box of 44 cookies. Today, the Girl Scouts sell approximately 200 million boxes every year. How many million have you snacked on?

Here are the Girl Scouts' best-selling cookies, starting with most popular:

1 **THIN MINTS**

2 **CARAMEL DELITES,** also called Samoas

3 **PEANUT BUTTER PATTIES,** also called Tagalongs

1912 ● **Juliette Gordon Low founds the Girl Scouts,** officially signing up the first 18 members in Savannah, Georgia. The mission of the Girl Scouts is to build "girls of courage, confidence, and character, who make the world a better place."

MARCH 13

1942 ● The U.S. military begins its new War Dog Program, known as the K-9 Corps. Dogs have always served a vital role in our military, helping soldiers detect dangers, delivering messages over dangerous terrain, and guarding bases against sneak attacks. To honor their service, every March 13 is celebrated as National K9 Veterans Day. Good patriotic doggies!

2003 ● **The journal *Nature* reports that researchers found 350,000-year-old footprints of Stone Age humans in Italy.** They were found on the side of a volcano, which makes you think these Stone Age dudes were probably running for their lives.

2022 ● Tom Brady, who retired a few weeks earlier, announces his unretirement from the NFL. Then at the end of the season, retires again. He is the most-winning quarterback in NFL history and holds the record for most Super Bowl victories (seven). Great at throwing, not so good at making up his mind.

★ It's Pi Day!

While it commemorates the mathematical constant 3.14 (the ratio of the circumference of any circle to the diameter of that circle), lots of people celebrate it with an actual pie. Who says math can't be tasty?

1879 Genius physicist Albert Einstein is born. His theories of special relativity (E=mc2) and general relativity drastically changed our understanding of how the universe works. While Einstein was obviously super book-smart, he also valued free and creative thinking above all. He once said, "Imagination is more important than knowledge. For knowledge is limited, whereas imagination embraces the entire world."

1889 Susan La Flesche Picotte becomes the first Native American to graduate from medical school in the United States. After graduating, she returned to the Nebraska Omaha Reservation, where she grew up, and dedicated her skills to helping her community. Eventually, she and her husband opened the first privately funded hospital on a reservation, where she said help was available to anyone who needed it, regardless of their race.

1950 The FBI releases the first Ten Most Wanted Fugitives list to make regular citizens aware of very bad guys and gals the FBI wants behind bars.

MARCH 15

44 BCE **Ever heard the expression *Beware the Ides of March*?** The Ides were a Roman celebration of the new year. But on this day, instead of partying, emperor Julius Caesar was stabbed to death by senators, including his friends Brutus and Cassius, who believed he was becoming too powerful. Great pals, huh?

1869 Play ball—and get paid! With 10 players on the payroll, the Cincinnati Red Stockings become baseball's first professional team. The highest-paid player, George Wright, made $1,400 that year.

2019 Inspired by 15-year-old Greta Thunberg, schoolchildren around the world join together in a day of climate-change protest. Greta has spoken about the environment at the United Nations, where she told leaders, "You are failing us" in protecting the world for future generations.

1802 • The first military school in the United States, known as West Point, is founded by Congress to educate and train future leaders of the U.S. Army. Many classmates who studied here went on to fight against one another in the Civil War.

1844 • An article in a London medical journal describes hay fever symptoms—the first time seasonal allergies are explained. The article called it "summer catarrh," which kind of sounds like someone trying to say something mid-sneeze.

1926 • The **first liquid-fuel rocket is launched** on a farm in Massachusetts. It flew for a total of two and a half seconds before landing in a cabbage field, so the celebration must have been brief.

MARCH 17

1601 • **The first recorded St. Patrick's Day parade is held,** marching through the Spanish-colonial town of St. Augustine, Florida. More than a hundred years later, homesick Irish soldiers marched in Boston and in New York City, starting a tradition that grew and grew. These days, the New York City St. Paddy's parade has 150,000 people marching and around 2 million people lining the streets to watch.

Four Lucky St. Patrick's Day Facts

1 The real St. Patrick was born in Britain, not Ireland.

2 Leprechauns are based on Celtic belief in fairies—tiny men and women with magical powers.

3 Shamrocks are so special in Ireland because they represent the arrival of spring. Most have three leaves, which is why finding a rare four-leaf clover is considered lucky.

4 The traditional St. Paddy's Day meal of corned beef and cabbage was popularized in America in the 1800s by impoverished Irish immigrants.

MARCH 18

1662 • The first public-bus system hits the streets of Paris with horse-powered vehicles. Literally. They were large carriages pulled by teams of horses.

1965 • Cosmonaut Alexei Leonov steps outside his spacecraft mid-flight—on purpose. Floating for 12 minutes, he became the first person to conduct a spacewalk. Don't look down, Alexei!

1966 • **A short-lived fad of "$1.25 disposable paper dresses" sees more than a million sold before people decide that the easily ripped clothes are indeed a rip-off.**

MARCH 19

1982 • A war between Argentina and the British empire over the Falkland Islands—or, as the Argentinians call them, Las Islas Malvinas—begins. After 12 weeks, Argentina surrenders.

2003 • Believing Iraqi dictator Saddam Hussein was making weapons of mass destruction, President George W. Bush announces that military operations have begun "to defend the world from grave danger." No WMDs were ever found, but Saddam Hussein was captured and arrested and found guilty of committing crimes against humanity.

MARCH 20

1800 • Italian inventor Alessandro Volta charges up the world as the inventor of the battery. Thank him next time you're on a long, boring car trip and have your phone to keep you entertained.

1966 • On this day, the World Cup trophy is stolen before the matches begin, and even after catching the thief, police can't find it. But a dog named Pickles saved the day. Out for a walk, Pickles kept sniffing at a parked car's tire. When Pickles' owner looked under the car to see what was up, he found the missing trophy. Pickles received a medal for his excellent detective work.

2013 • **The first U.N. International Day of Happiness is celebrated.** The day serves as a reminder to all world leaders to prioritize giving people the support they need to live happy and productive lives.

It's World Poetry Day!

Roses are red, violets are blue, we wrote a poem on World Poetry Day, and so can you!

1999 • Talk about high aspirations—after 20 days in flight, adventurers **Bertrand Piccard and Brian Jones become the first to travel around the world nonstop in a hot-air balloon.**

2006 • **The first tweet is tweeted on Twitter (now called X).** For such a historic event for a platform that will change the landscape of social media, it's honestly kind of lame. Sent by founder Jack Dorsey, it simply reads, "just setting up my twttr."

MARCH 22

_923 • **Marcel Marceau, the famous French mime, is born.** Pretend to blow out candles on an imaginary cake in his honor!

_993 • The first World Water Day is observed. Held every year, the day is designed to raise awareness of the 2.2 billion people living without access to safe drinking water.

_995 • Cosmonaut Valeri Polyakova returns to earth after staying aboard the Mir space station for nearly 438 days, the longest stay in space. Many astronauts and cosmonauts say it is super weird during their first few days back on earth to have to remember that if they drop something, it will fall rather than float midair.

MARCH 23

1839 • The initials "O.K." are first published in *The Boston Morning Post*. It stands for "oll korrect," which obviously isn't correct, but it catches on. Are you OK with that?

1983 • The real *Star Wars*: President Ronald Reagan announces the Strategic Defense Initiative, which could use X-ray lasers fired from outer space to destroy any nuclear missiles headed toward the United States. If that sounds a little far-fetched, that's because it was. The system was never actually made but was most likely announced to scare the Soviet Union.

2018 • A massive sandstorm blows from the Sahara all the way to Sochi, Russia, turning the snow slopes bright orange. Pretty—and *pretty* weird!

2021 • **The Ever Given, an enormous freight boat, turns sideways in the Suez Canal and gets stuck** for nearly a week. The blockade caused monthslong shipping delays of everything from computers to cars.

MARCH 24

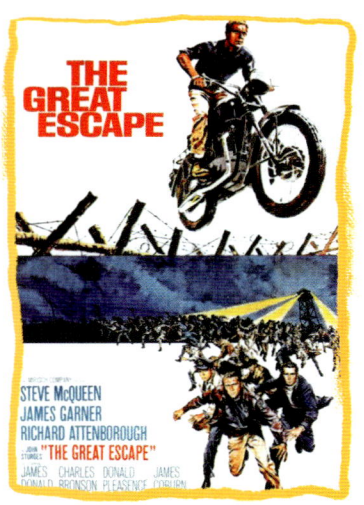

1944 • After a year of secretly digging, **76 Allied prisoners escape from a German prisoner-of-war camp through a 333-foot-long tunnel. It was one of the most daring escapes ever and the basis of the film *The Great Escape*.** Sadly, unlike in the movie, most of the escapees were recaptured by the Germans. Only three were lucky enough to make it out for good.

1989 • One of the worst oil spills in history happens when the supertanker *Exxon Valdez* hits a reef in Prince William Sound in Alaska. About 11 million gallons of oil went into the water, polluting more than 700 miles of the coastline and harming hundreds of thousands of birds, fish, and mammals.

1863 — The first Medal of Honor, the highest award someone in the U.S. military can receive, is given to Army Pvt. Jacob Parrott, who was a part of a dangerous covert raid against the Confederate Army. Since 1990, Congress has declared every March 25 as National Medal of Honor Day to thank those who have performed a personal act of valor above and beyond the call of duty.

1911 — A terrible fire breaks out at the Triangle Shirtwaist Company factory in New York City, tragically killing 146 workers. The horrible event led to new laws and regulations designed to protect the safety of factory workers.

1954 — **RCA begins manufacturing the first mass-produced color TV.** The screen is 15 inches, and it cost $1,000, which equals about $9,800 in today's money.

1965 — A group of 3,200 civil rights demonstrators led by Martin Luther King Jr. complete a march from Selma to Montgomery, Alabama. National Guardsmen and FBI agents were there to protect the safety of the marchers, who had been turned back twice by Alabama state police officers at Selma's Edmund Pettus Bridge. The march was watched by millions on TV and helped pave the way for the Voting Rights Act to be signed into law.

MARCH 26

1953 — Physician and medical researcher Jonas Salk announces his vaccine for the crippling disease of polio. In 1952, 58,000 new cases were reported in the United States. Salk's vaccine effectively wiped out the disease. Since 2009, there had been zero polio cases originating in the U.S. until an unvaccinated adult contracted it in 2022.

2012 — **The 12-year-old skateboarder Tom Schaar performs the first successfully landed 1080** (which is three full rotations in the air). After five tries at the MegaRamp at Woodward West action sports camp in Tehachapi, California, he nailed it. "It was the hardest trick I've ever done, but it was easier than I thought," Schaar told ESPN.

MARCH 27

1915 — A domestic servant named Mary Mallon, better known as Typhoid Mary, is placed under permanent quarantine. Mary was a carrier of the disease typhoid but was immune to its effects. She never got sick from it, but she passed it on to people who presumably passed it on to others. Investigators believe she was the source of 120 infections—and five deaths.

1968 — New sport alert! Hoyle Schweitzer and Jim Drake file a patent for the Windsurfer sailboard a surfboard that has a mast and sail attached to it. Windsurfing (literally) takes off and has several pro leagues. These things can move 40 mph in the right conditions, so hold on!

1975 — Construction on the Alaska Pipeline begins. The pipeline is exactly what it sounds like, a massive pipe that runs both above and below ground for 800 miles carrying oil from northern Alaskan fields southward.

MARCH 28

1891 — The first world weightlifting championship contest is held. We're going to guess that the contest's winner, Edward Lawrence Levy, had no trouble lifting his trophy.

1979 — The worst nuclear accident in U.S. history occurs at Three Mile Island, a small island in the Susquehanna River in Pennsylvania. While there were no known health effects to humans, animals, or plant life in the area, the accident caused fear of a nuclear catastrophe and public distrust of nuclear-plant safety.

2011 — **Alain Robert, also known as the French Spider-Man, climbs up the outside of the world's tallest skyscraper.** It takes him six hours to scale the 2,717-foot Burj Khalifa tower in Dubai. Next time, try the elevator?

MARCH 29

1973 — The last U.S. combat troops leave Vietnam, effectively ending the Vietnam War. The war pitted Communist North Vietnam against South Vietnam and the U.S. Two years after the U.S. withdrew most of its troops, North and South Vietnam reunited under Communist rule.

1974 — Farmers in Xian, China, discover an ancient tomb that contains amazing artifacts, including more than 8,000 life-size clay soldiers. This terra-cotta army had been put in place to guard the burial site of China's first emperor, Qin Shi Huang Di, and the men have been standing at attention for more than 2,000 years. Someone, get these guys a chair!

1842 • The first use of an anesthetic, called ether, is used in surgery. We're sure the patient was happy to snooze through it.

1923 • The ocean liner RMS *Laconia* is the first passenger cruise ship to circle the world, taking 130 days to make the round trip.

1939 • Watch out, bad guys! **Batman makes his first appearance in *Detective Comics* #27.** (Robin didn't show up until the next year—that kid is always late!)

The Batman Fact File

1 Batman's original creators were Bob Kane and Bill Finger.

2 Batman's real identity, Bruce Wayne, is a combination of two historical figures: Robert the Bruce (the Scottish warrior king who defeated the English) and Anthony Wayne (a fierce commander for the Continental Army in the Revolutionary War).

3 Batman never uses guns and has a no-kill policy.

4 Batman carries kryptonite with him at all times in case Superman goes crazy.

5 Luke Skywalker was the Joker. Actor Mark Hamill, who played the ultimate good guy in *Star Wars*, voiced the ultimate bad guy in *Batman: The Animated Series*.

MARCH 31

1889 • *Ooh la la!* The Eiffel Tower officially opens. The 984-foot structure was designed by Gustave Eiffel, who also created the internal support structure of the Statue of Liberty.

2020 • Prince Harry and Meghan Markle trade in their crowns for surfboards. The Duke and Duchess of Sussex officially quit their lives as royals and moved to California. The only castles they'll have now are ones they make on the beach with their kids.

★ It's National Crayon Day!

The most famous crayon brand, Crayola, was started in 1903. The first box sold had eight colors and cost a nickel. Today, Crayolas come in 120 colors, and the company makes over 3 billion of them a year.

THIS DAY IN *my* HISTORY
MARCH

Fill in any memorable events from your life here.

1 ....

2 ....

3 ....

4 ....

5 ....

6 ....

7 ....

8 ....

9 ....

10 ....

11 ....

12 ....

13 ....

14 ....

15 ....

16 ....

17 ....

18 ....

19 ....

20 ....

21 ....

22 ....

23 ....

24 ....

25 ....

26 ....

27 ....

28 ....

29 ....

30 ....

31 ....

NOTHING INTERESTING EVER HAPPENS ON THIS DAY. JUST KIDDING—APRIL FOOLS! No one is totally sure when this day became an annual holiday for pulling pranks and tricks, but one thing is for certain, don't believe anything anyone says on April 1!

1976 College dropouts **Steve Wozniak and Steve Jobs found Apple Computer in Jobs' parents' garage.** The first Apples they sold didn't come with a monitor, a keyboard, or even a casing around the computer's guts. Jeez, guess we shouldn't complain so much when Apple decides to randomly change the power ports every few years.

2001 Love is love! Just after midnight, the mayor of Amsterdam, Job Cohen, married four couples in city hall, making the Netherlands the first country in the world to legalize same-sex marriages.

APRIL 2

1805 Crack open your favorite book from first grade—it's International Children's Book Day, which is celebrated every year on the birthday of fairy-tale writer Hans Christian Andersen. He's the guy who wrote famous stories like "The Little Mermaid," "The Emperor's New Clothes," and "The Ugly Duckling."

1877 **Circus performer Rossa Matilda Richter is the first human to be shot out of a cannon.** It's even more amazing to think that there was a second person who wanted to do that.

1917 Jeannette Rankin of Montana is sworn in, becoming the first woman elected to Congress. Rankin pledged to work for a constitutional amendment guaranteeing women's right to vote. A pacifist, she was the only member of Congress to vote no on the U.S. getting involved in World War I and World War II.

1931 Seventeen-year-old left-handed female pitcher Jackie Mitchell pitches against the New York Yankees in two exhibition games and strikes out superstar hitters Lou Gehrig and Babe Ruth.

APRIL 3

1860 — The first Pony Express mail, traveling by horse and rider relay teams, gallops off. The mail packet left St. Joseph, Missouri, and, 10 days later, arrived 1,800 miles away in Sacramento, California. While not exactly same-day shipping, it was the fastest way to communicate and ship long distances before the telegraph or the transcontinental railroad began operation.

1934 — We're not monkeying around: **Jane Goodall is born!**

1973 — Motorola employee Martin Cooper makes the first cell call in history. Standing in downtown New York City, he dials Bell Labs headquarters in New Jersey. Asked what he said in that world-changing exchange, Cooper replied, "'I'm ringing you just to see if my call sounds good at your end,' or something to that effect." Wow, quite the conversationalist.

Who Is Jane Goodall?

Dr. Jane Goodall's work studying chimpanzees for many decades in the Gombe Stream National Park of Tanzania made her the most famous primatologist in the world. She had many groundbreaking observations of the animals, including witnessing chimpanzees using tools (people thought only humans did that). Today, Goodall is a fierce fighter for the protection of animals and their habitats.

APRIL 4

It's National School Librarian Day!

Whisper your appreciation, then *shush*!

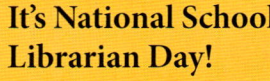

1928 — Today is the birthday of world-famous poet, performer, activist, and scholar Maya Angelou. One of her most famous poems, "Still I Rise," begins with these inspiring words: "You may write me down in history / With your bitter, twisted lies, / You may trod me in the very dirt / But still, like dust, I'll rise."

1975 — Bill Gates and Paul Allen found the computer software company Microsoft. Twelve years later, 31-year-old Gates became the world's youngest billionaire. Guess that means it was a success.

1722 • **Jacob Roggeveen is the first European to visit Easter Island**, located in the South Pacific.

What's Up With Those Giant Statues?

Easter Island (called Rapa Nui by its initial Polynesian population) is home to nearly 900 giant stone statues situated all around the island. They average about 13 feet tall and weigh about 13 tons. Carved as early as 700 CE, archaeologists have not yet figured out why these statues were made or how such heavy creations were moved around the island. We're going to guess that hernias were pretty common on Rapa Nui back then.

1951 • Julius and Ethel Rosenberg, who were convicted as spies passing U.S. atomic secrets to the Soviets, were sentenced to death. They were the first and only U.S. citizens to be executed for espionage during peacetime.

APRIL 6

1772 • Good news for Santa Claus on this day: Russian leader Catherine the Great abolishes a tax on beards. Wait, what? Yes, in a wacky effort to modernize his country, the nation's earlier leader Peter the Great tried to get men to shave off their beards by making them pay to have fluffy faces.

1896 • **The first modern Olympics kicks off** 1,500 years after they were banned by Roman Emperor Theodosius I. The games took place in Greece and featured athletes from 12 countries. The star of the show? Greek runner Spyridon Louis, who won the first-ever Olympic marathon.

1909 • **American explorer Robert Peary, his Black assistant Matthew Henson, and four Inuit hunters are the first to reach the North Pole**...sort of. Decades after Peary's death, experts examined his travel log and determined the expedition was likely a few miles short of its goal. Close enough if you ask us.

APRIL 7

1913 • Next time you grab a cold juice box, thank Fred Wolf, who patented the first successful refrigerator that was small enough to fit in people's kitchens.

1927 • Long before Zoom calls, future president of the United States Herbert Hoover makes the first public demonstration of a video phone call. Wonder if he forgot to unmute himself.

1969 • This day marks the Internet's symbolic birthday, when the first-ever RFC (Request for Comments) was posted. Translated into language we can understand, that means engineers shared research and asked other engineers for feedback. Imagine the world's nerdiest chat room.

2007 • Ultra swimmer Martin Strel finishes swimming the entire length of the Amazon River—3,273.38 miles. The two-month journey started in Peru and ended in Brazil. Luckily, he had plenty of piranhas to keep him company.

2020 • Tony Fisher temporarily grabs a spot in the *Guinness Book of World Records* by building the largest functioning Rubik's Cube. It's six feet seven inches tall and really works! But you don't just need a lot of brain power to solve it; you need a lot of muscle. To make vertical spins, you must flip the entire cube over.

★ It's National Burrito Day!

In Spanish *burrito* means "little donkey." They were likely given this name because they look like bedrolls that donkeys carried on their backs in the 1800s. Um, we just lost our appetite.

ORIGINS of the BURRITO

APRIL 8

NOW YOU SEE ME, NOW YOU DON'T!

1974 • Baseball superstar Hank Aaron was nicknamed Hammerin' Hank, and here's why: He hammered *a lot* of baseballs out of the park, a total of 755 before he retired. On this day, he hit his 715th home run, beating Babe Ruth's record. His record stood until 2007 when Barry Bonds broke it, but Bonds later admitted to using steroids, so many people say Hammerin' Hank is still the record holder.

1983 • **Magician David Copperfield wows the world by making the Statue of Liberty appear to disappear.** Thankfully, he put it back.

1860 French inventor **Édouard-Léon Scott de Martinville records himself singing using what he calls a phonautograph,** which traced sound waves onto paper that was blackened by smoke. Then 150 years later, scientists figured out a way to listen to it, making it the oldest voice recording. Put him on *The Voice*!

1865 Confederate General Robert E. Lee surrenders to U.S. Lieutenant General Ulysses S. Grant at the Appomattox Court House in Virginia, finally ending the Civil War after four years. It was the deadliest war in American history, with approximately 620,000 soldiers left dead at the hands of their fellow countrymen.

APRIL 10

1849 The safety pin is patented. And possibly the word *ouch*!

1866 The American Society for the Prevention of Cruelty to Animals (ASPCA) is founded in New York City, and it is still hard at work today. Thanks to their work, approximately 4.1 million shelter animals are adopted each year (2 million dogs and 2.1 million cats). That's a lot of happy wagging tails!

1872 More trees please! **The first Arbor Day in America is celebrated,** founded by J. Sterling Morton to encourage people to plant trees in Nebraska, which was mostly prairie and farmland. Prizes were offered to those who planted the most trees, and some estimates say more than 1 million trees were planted on that first Arbor Day. Great news for people seeking shade; bad news for people who have to rake leaves.

1953 The first color 3D movie, *House of Wax*, premieres in New York City. The horror movie thrilled audiences (when they were brave enough to keep their eyes open).

1998 The Belfast Agreement (also known as the Good Friday Agreement) ends 30 years of bloody conflict over who governed Northern Ireland. It was approved by public votes in Northern Ireland and the Republic of Ireland, and ended the period known as the Troubles, in which at least 3,500 people were killed.

APRIL 11

1970 — "Houston, we've had a problem." These were the words that *Apollo 13* commander James Lovell said three days after the mission's launch on April 11, 1970. While 205,000 miles from earth, the *Apollo* spacecraft experienced a sudden loss in power. The crew had no heat and very little light, but nerves of steel. Through their determination and with the fast-thinking problem solvers at mission control in Houston, the astronauts ultimately safely returned to earth in one of the most remarkable survival stories in history.

2010 — Like in the movie *Up* but in real life, **U.S. pilot Jonathan Trappe flies for 109 miles over North Carolina using a cluster of 57 giant balloons.** He soared 7,474 feet above the ground, which lets us know that this dude wasn't afraid of heights or mischievous birds popping his balloons for fun.

APRIL 12

1861 — The Civil War begins as Confederate guns and mortars open fire on the Union-held Fort Sumter in Charleston Harbor, South Carolina. President Lincoln had actually asked Robert E. Lee to command the Union forces, but Lee was loyal to Virginia and led the army of the South.

1961 — Cosmonaut Yuri Gagarin becomes the first person to travel to space. When returning to earth, Gagarin ejected himself from the space capsule and floated down with a parachute. Some sources report a farmer and her granddaughter were stunned to see this strange man land near them in a bright orange suit, as Gagarin later recalled: "When they saw me in my space suit and the parachute dragging alongside as I walked, they started to back away in fear. I told them, 'Don't be afraid, I am a Soviet like you, who has descended from space, and I must find a telephone to call Moscow!'"

2009 — After four days of being held captive by Somali pirates operating in the Indian Ocean, a freight ship captain named Richard Phillips is saved by Navy SEALs in one of the most amazing hostage rescues ever.

2017 — Upon stepping on the North Pole, 20-year-old **Marin Minamiya becomes the youngest person to complete the Explorer's Grand Slam**—the challenge to climb the world's Seven Summits and reach the North and South Pole.

1953 — The most famous spy springs to life, and his name is "Bond, James Bond." Agent 007 first appeared as the hero in the novel *Casino Royale* written by Ian Fleming. As of 2022, he has been the world-saving, gadget-loving super-spy in 25 official movies and been portrayed by six different actors.

1997 — **Fore! A 21-year-old golfer named Tiger Woods wins the Masters Tournament by a record 12 strokes in Augusta, Georgia.** He was also the first person of either Asian or African heritage to win one of the four major tournaments.

2016 — The Golden State Warriors defeat the Memphis Grizzlies, 125-104, for their 73rd win, which also defeats Michael Jordan's Chicago Bulls' record for the most wins in a single season. Having three-point shooting legend Steph Curry on your team sure helps!

2019 — The *Stratolaunch*, the world's largest aircraft by wingspan, takes flight. From wingtip to wingtip, it is longer than a football field. Why is it so big? The *Stratolaunch* was made to carry rockets to launch commercial satellites into space. (Rockets are not things that will easily fit into the overhead compartment of a typical plane.)

❓ Did You Know?

Wonder why golfers yell "Fore!" when they're about to tee off? In the 1700s and 1800s, a person called a forecaddie would walk ahead and hang out where the balls were likely to land, so they didn't get lost. Over time, *forecaddie* likely got shortened to *fore* and became a warning to watch out.

APRIL 14

1865 — While watching a play at Ford's Theatre in Washington, D.C., President Abraham Lincoln is assassinated by Confederate sympathizer John Wilkes Booth.

1981 — The first space shuttle, *Columbia*, touches down on a dry lake bed at Edwards Air Force Base. This is the first NASA mission that ends with a wheeled landing in a spacecraft that could be reused. The Space Shuttle Program flew 135 missions over four decades until space shuttle *Atlantis* rolled to a stop on the runway on July 21, 2011.

2010 — A massive volcano eruption in Iceland sends so much debris into the sky that it shuts down air travel in Europe for nearly a week. Even harder than trying to see through all the ash is trying to say the volcano's name: Eyjafjallajökull.

APRIL 15

1452 — World Art Day is celebrated today on the birthday of famous artist Leonardo da Vinci.

1912 — The "unsinkable" ship RMS *Titanic* sinks after hitting an iceberg. Between 1,490 and 1,635 people perished in the disaster.

1947 — **Jackie Robinson makes his historic debut in front of Brooklyn Dodgers fans at Ebbets Field**; it is the first time a Black athlete is playing in a Major League Baseball game. Since 2009, to honor this great moment, every professional baseball player wears his number—42—on their jersey on Jackie Robinson Day.

1955 — Entrepreneur Ray Kroc opens his first McDonald's franchise. The original menu had only nine items: hamburger, cheeseburger, fries, shake, Coke, root beer, orange drink, coffee, and milk. Even smaller than the menu were the prices—a cheeseburger was 19 cents!

2020 — Scientists in India name a new species of green snake after the *Harry Potter* character Salazar Slytherin: It's called the *Trimeresurus salazar* or Salazar's pit viper

APRIL 16

2003 — **Michael Jordan plays his last game in the NBA.** But for real this time. See, Jordan retired twice before but kept coming back. Here are just some numbers that show why he is considered by most NBA fans to be the GOAT (greatest of all time):

- **6 NBA CHAMPIONSHIPS**
- **5 REGULAR SEASON MOST VALUABLE PLAYER AWARDS**
- **6 FINALS MVP AWARDS**
- **2 SLAM DUNK CHAMPIONSHIPS**
- **2 OLYMPIC GOLD MEDALS**
- **1 PRESIDENTIAL MEDAL OF FREEDOM**

2018 — The Pulitzer Prize for music is awarded to rapper Kendrick Lamar for his 2017 album *DAMN*. It's the first time the award went to a hip-hop artist.

1961 • Trained by the CIA, 1,400 Cuban exiles launch an invasion at Cuba's Bay of Pigs to overthrow communist dictator Fidel Castro. The mission was a complete failure and further strained the tension between the U.S. and Cuba.

1964 • **The Ford Mustang revs its engine for the first time at the World's Fair.** It becomes an icon of American muscle cars and the best-selling sports car in the world.

1993 • Dr. Ellen Ochoa glides to a landing as a crew member of the space shuttle *Discovery*, becoming the first Hispanic American woman who went to space. She traveled to space three more times and logged nearly 1,000 hours in orbit before hanging up her space suit.

APRIL **18**

1775 • Paul Revere, William Dawes, Samuel Prescott, and other colonists join a midnight horseback ride from Charlestown to Lexington warning their compatriots that an attack from the British army is underway. They yelled at the top of their lungs, "The regulars are coming! The regulars are coming!" That's right, they didn't say, "The British are coming!" as most people think. That wouldn't have made any sense because all of the colonists were British too!

1906 • A massive earthquake hits, violently shaking San Francisco for nearly a full minute. The destruction causes a massive fire that kills more than 3,000 people. When it is all over, 75 percent of the city lies in charred rubble.

1938 • Cocreated by Joe Shuster and Jerry Siegel, **the new superhero Superman is copyrighted.** Supes appeared for first time in *Action Comics* #1 and became the most famous superhero of all time, fighting for truth, justice, and the American way. But it almost didn't happen! Shuster and Siegel's original idea was that Superman would be a villain!

2018 • After a 35-year ban by conservative religious leaders, movies are once again allowed to be played in cinemas in Saudi Arabia. The first movie shown in theaters is *Black Panther*.

APRIL 19

1897 — John J. McDermott wins the first Boston Marathon in 2:55:10. The world's oldest annual marathon, it was inspired by the, well, runaway success of the first marathon at the 1896 Summer Olympics.

1987 — The Simpsons make their TV debut in a short film called *Good Night* on *The Tracey Ullman Show*. Then, in 1989, *The Simpsons* became its own show. By 2018 it had taken over *Gunsmoke*'s record for the longest-running scripted show in TV history. As Bart would say, "Eat my shorts, *Gunsmoke*!"

2021 — After unhitching from the Perseverance rover on Mars, **NASA's *Ingenuity* helicopter takes off**, performing the first powered flight on another planet in history.

I'M FLYING!

APRIL 20

1961 — The first Iron Man is named...Harold? On this day, **pilot and inventor Harold "Hal" Graham completes the first jet-pack flight.** It took him only 18 inches off the ground and carried him 112 feet (less than half a city block)—but still, it worked!

2008 — Race car driver Danica Patrick wins the Indy Japan 300, making her the first female driver in history to get the checkered flag at an IndyCar Series race.

2010 — The offshore oil rig Deepwater Horizon explodes, resulting in the largest ocean oil spill in history. The oil slick covered 57,500 square miles in the Gulf of Mexico, bigger than the entire state of Pennsylvania.

What Is BC, AD, BCE, and CE?

Historians have used the birth of Jesus as a marker for dating events. Anything that happened before that is labeled BC ("before Christ"), and anything after is AD (*anno Domini*, Latin for "in the year of the Lord"). A more secular way of noting dates (meaning, a method that isn't tied to religion) is using BCE ("before the Common Era") and CE ("Common Era"). But whatever you choose, the dates are the same: 100 BC is 100 BCE; 100 AD is 100 CE.

753 BCE • According to legend, Rome is founded on this date by orphaned twins Remus and Romulus on the site where a she-wolf fed them milk. The wolf part is a little unbelievable, but Rome became a true empire—1.7 million square miles spread out over three continents.

2015 • **A test train for the Shinkansen, Japan's high-speed rail system, reaches a top speed of 375 mph**, breaking the record for the fastest rail vehicle. Japan's bullet trains are used every day by commuters... who are apparently in a very big rush.

APRIL 22

1915 • **Deadly gas is used as a weapon for the first time by the German army in World War I.** Gas attacks were particularly heinous, irritating the lungs and causing choking and death. It is estimated that 500,000 troops were injured by gas during WWI. That's why American troops in the 102nd Infantry were lucky to have Sergeant Stubby in their ranks. Stubby was a dog who traveled from America with the troops, and after surviving a gas attack, his nose became very sensitive to the smell of gas. Stubby would bark when he got a whiff of it, which warned his fellow troopers to put on gas masks long before the fumes arrived in deadly concentration.

STUBBY

1970 • **The first Earth Day is held.** It's like a big birthday party for our world to increase environmental awareness and sustainability efforts. Can a planet blow out birthday candles?

IT'S MY BIRTHDAY!

APRIL 23

1976
The world gets a little louder with the release of the first album by the Ramones. The group, made up of four guys from Queens, New York, helped launch a new form of music called punk rock. The sound is fast, loud, super catchy, and often has goofy, sarcastic lyrics meant to poke fun at social norms. ("I Wanna Be Sedated" was one of their big hits.) The Ramones influenced tons of today's bands, from Green Day to Metallica.

1985
Coca-Cola Company's New Coke launches big and quickly fizzes out. The company released a new formula meant to replace the original flavor, and the public freaked out. Massive letter-writing campaigns and public outcry led the company to bring back Coca-Cola Classic less than three months later.

2005
YouTube gets its first video upload. Titled "Me at the Zoo," it features YouTube cofounder Jawed Karim talking for 18 seconds in front of an elephant exhibit. By early 2023, it had been watched more than 246 million times.

APRIL 24

1184 BCE
The Trojan War between the Greeks and defenders of the city of Troy ends with the sneakiest sneak attack ever. The Greeks, in an apparent sign that they were done fighting, departed in ships and left behind a giant wooden horse at the city gates as a victory offering. The triumphant Trojan army happily took it inside their city walls. But little did they know, Greek soldiers were hiding inside the horse, and they climbed out in the middle of the night to take over the city. That's the story anyway. Historians debate whether the Trojan horse story is myth or reality—but no one can argue that it wasn't a clever idea!

1996
"We Got Next!" The NBA Board of Governors approves the Women's National Basketball Association—the WNBA—which begins wowing hoops fans when games tip off in June of 1997.

⭐ It's World Penguin Day!

Here are some amazing facts about these funny, wobbly wonders:

- There are 18 different types of penguins.

- Blue penguins are the tiniest, growing only 12 to 13 inches tall.

- Emperor penguins are the largest and can stand over four feet tall.

- Their black-and-white coloring is perfect camouflage when swimming. From above, their black backs blend into the sea floor, and from below, their white bellies get lost in the brightness of the ocean's surface.

- While they look clumsy on land, penguins are remarkable swimmers that can reach speeds of 22 mph.

- Penguins can't fly, but tiny Adélie penguins can launch themselves nine feet in the air from the water to get back on dry land.

1944 The first time a helicopter is used in combat. During World War II, pilot Lieutenant Carter Harmon used a YB-4B helicopter to rescue four men who had crash-landed in Japanese territory. Harmon received the Distinguished Flying Cross for his daring and heroic mission.

1990 **The Hubble Space Telescope deploys into orbit from the space shuttle *Discovery*.** Clouds and light pollution are no longer a problem for astronomers, who now have a crystal-clear view of distant stars and galaxies from the telescope that lives in space.

APRIL **26**

1803 The scientific community finally accepts that meteorites from outer space are real when more than 3,000 rocks rain down on the city of L'Aigle in France. How do you say, "Put on a helmet!" in French?

1941 Da-da-daaa-daaa! **Baseball fans at Wrigley Field are the first to be entertained by live organ music between innings.**

1986 An explosion at the Chernobyl nuclear power plant in the then-Soviet Union (now Ukraine) pollutes the area with about 400 times more radioactive material than the atomic bombs dropped on Hiroshima and Nagasaki combined.

APRIL 27

1956 · World Heavyweight Champion boxer Rocky Marciano retires with an undefeated record of 49-0. He's the only heavyweight in history with a perfect record. Funnily enough, he didn't want to be a boxer. He really wanted to be a baseball player but got cut by the Cubs.

2006 · Construction of the Freedom Tower begins at the site of the Twin Towers 9/11 terrorist attack. In November 2014, the tower, officially named One World Trade Center, opens alongside the memorial to those who died in the attack.

2011 · A complete weather nightmare: 216 tornadoes hit 26 states in the U.S.

APRIL 28

1947 · Six men pile onto a balsa-wood raft called *Kon-Tiki* on the shore of Peru. One hundred and one days later, they arrived in Polynesia, 4,300 miles away, proving that ancient South Americans could have sailed to that part of the world.

TOURISTS...

2001 · U.S. millionaire Dennis Tito travels to the International Space Station, becoming the first space tourist. Hope he had a good time up there because the flight was not cheap: He paid $20 million for the experience, which he later said was "the greatest moment of my life."

APRIL 29

1429 • During the 100 Years War between England and France, 17-year-old **Joan of Arc leads the French army to free the city of Orleans.** In 1431 she was captured by the English, who accused the passionate leader of being a witch and burned her to death at the stake.

2010 • *Time* magazine names animal behaviorist, writer, and industrial designer Temple Grandin on its list of the 100 most influential people. Dr. Grandin was born with autism and uses her unique insights into what makes living creatures comfortable and uncomfortable to develop new ways to reduce stress.

2013 • Washington Wizards center Jason Collins proudly tells the world he is gay, becoming the first active player in a major U.S. professional sports league to come out publicly.

APRIL 30

1006 • **The brightest supernova observed in history lights up the night sky.** (A supernova is a star exploding at the end of its life cycle.) The explosion was so big that it was seen by people in Asia, the Middle East, and Europe.

1789 • George Washington is inaugurated as the first president of the United States of America. Unlike today's politicians, who usually brag about how great they are, Washington opened his inaugural address by saying he was terrified of the job he was just given and thought he was a terrible choice for it.

1888 • In Moradabad, India, the deadliest hailstorm ever recorded happens. The hailstones, some reportedly as large as goose eggs and oranges, killed 246 people.

1993 • An organization called CERH releases software that makes the World Wide Web accessible to the public. In other words, **the Internet is born!**

What the Heck Is Hail?

Hailstones form when raindrops are carried by thunderstorm updrafts into super cold areas of the atmosphere. They freeze and grow in size as more water collides and sticks to them. Eventually, the hailstones fall when they are too heavy to be supported by the thunderstorm updraft.

THIS DAY IN *my* HISTORY
APRIL

Fill in any memorable events from your life here.

1 ....
2 ....
3 ....
4 ....
5 ....
6 ....
7 ....
8 ....
9 ....
10 ....
11 ....
12 ....
13 ....
14 ....
15 ....

16 ....
17 ....
18 ....
19 ....
20 ....
21 ....
22 ....
23 ....
24 ....
25 ....
26 ....
27 ....
28 ....
29 ....
30 ....

IT'S ASIAN AMERICAN AND PACIFIC ISLANDER HERITAGE MONTH! The month is meant to raise awareness of API accomplishments and culture in America and celebrate them. May was chosen in part because the first Japanese immigrant, Manjiro, a 14-year-old boy, arrived in the United States on May 7, 1843, and the transcontinental railroad, built mainly by Chinese immigrants, was completed on May 10, 1869.

1931 • With the press of a button in the White House, President Herbert Hoover switches on the lights of the Empire State Building in New York City, officially opening what was then the world's tallest skyscraper.

1962 • **Hulk smash! The big guy makes his first appearance in *The Incredible Hulk* #1.** He was a bit different than the Hulk we know today: He was gray, not green. And Bruce Banner didn't transform when he got angry—he turned into the Hulk simply when day turned to night. Hulk afraid of dark?

1984 • The first issue of *Teenage Mutant Ninja Turtles* comes out. Written and drawn by Kevin Eastman and Peter Laird, the comic book was printed using a $1,000 loan from Eastman's uncle. (Something tells us Michelangelo would have used that $1,000 to buy pizza.)

1999 • A funny, oddly shaped character pops up on Nickelodeon for the first time. His name? **SpongeBob SquarePants.**

What Are Constellations?

Constellations are groups of stars that look like objects, people, or animals. The IAU's list of 88 official constellations come from ancient Greek astronomers, who brought together ideas from Babylonian, Egyptian, and Assyrian stargazers. Basically, staring up at stars and imagining stories was like watching TV for ancient folks.

SHH! IT'S BACK ON!

1922 — **The International Astronomical Union (IAU) releases its official list of 88 constellations that can be seen in the night sky.** In the northern hemisphere, you can see 36 of them. The remaining 52 require a trip below the equator to peep.

1933 — Scottish newspaper the *Inverness Courier* tells the story of a couple who claim they saw an enormous animal "rolling and plunging" on the surface of a lake called Loch Ness. And so was born the legend of the Loch Ness Monster.

2008 — The first film in the Marvel Cinematic Universe, *Iron Man*, takes off. Bad guys and box-office records were no match for Iron Man's repulsor blasts.

2011 — Osama bin Laden, leader of the terrorist group al-Qaeda that carried out the 9/11 attacks 10 years earlier, is shot and killed at his compound in Abbottabad, Pakistan, by United States Navy SEALs.

MAY 3

1971 — National Public Radio (NPR) begins its flagship newscast, reporting on the Vietnam War protests. At its start, fewer than 2 million people listened to NPR. More than 50 years later, more than 60 million listen to its broadcasts through its massive network of member stations.

1978 — The first spam email is sent by a guy named Gary Thuerk, who blasts a computer sales message to a few hundred people on ARPANET (the computer network that predated the Internet.) Gary's sales technique caught on, and these days an estimated 319.6 billion spam emails are sent every day!

It's National Teacher's Day!

Ever hear of the old tradition of giving a teacher an apple? Historians believe that kids in early America did this because families of school-age children were responsible for housing and feeding frontier teachers. Imagine telling your teacher there'll be no dinner if they give you too much homework?

⭐ It's *Star Wars* Day!

"MAY THE FOURTH BE WITH YOU!" (Say it out loud if you don't get it.)

❓ Did You Know?

The first *Star Wars* movie was almost *really, really, really* long. When George Lucas started writing it in the 1970s, he realized the story he wanted to tell would make people have to sit in a movie theater for eight hours. So he chopped his story into three parts that each turned into their own movie: *A New Hope*, *The Empire Strikes Back*, and *Return of the Jedi*. Plus, he knew way back then that he'd want to make prequels, which is why the first *Star Wars* movie's opening title sequence says "Episode 4."

1979 • **Margaret Thatcher takes office as the first woman to be elected prime minister of the United Kingdom.** She earned the nickname the Iron Lady because of her strong and tough leadership style.

MAY 5

1862 • **The Mexican army defeats the French in the Battle of Puebla on this day, Cinco de Mayo, which translates to "fifth of May."** Lots of people mistakenly think it is Mexican Independence Day. In Mexico, Cinco de Mayo actually isn't a big deal, but in America it has become a huge celebration of Mexican culture with traditional music, dancing, food, and drink.

1904 • Baseball team Boston American's pitcher Cy Young pitches the first perfect game of major league baseball's modern era against the Philadelphia Athletics. That means over the course of nine innings, not one Philly player got on base—they either struck out, flew out, or grounded out. Every year, the MLB gives the Cy Young Award to the best pitcher in the National and American Leagues.

MARACA

1961 • Navy Commander Alan Bartlett Shepard Jr. is the first American astronaut to travel into space. He's out there for only 15 minutes, and 10 years later he goes back for more—and plays golf on the surface of the moon.

MAY 6

1882 President Chester A. Arthur signs the Chinese Exclusion Act, initially a 10-year ban on Chinese laborers coming to the United States. Many Americans blamed their lower wages and overall money problems on lower-paid Chinese workers. Chinese immigrants were unable to become citizens until 1943. In 2011, Congress condemned the Chinese Exclusion Act as a violation of civil rights and constitutional protections.

1937 German airship *Hindenburg*, a giant hydrogen-filled blimp-like flying machine, bursts into flames and crashes while trying to dock in New Jersey. Thirteen passengers, 22 crew members, and one civilian from the ground crew lost their lives, and most of the survivors suffered terrible injuries. Radio announcer Herb Morrison was on the scene and gave one of the most famous live broadcasts in radio history as he watched the airship incinerate before his eyes, shouting despairingly, "Oh, the humanity!"

1954 Run, Roger, run! Twenty-five-year-old Roger Bannister is the first runner to crack the four-minute mile, winning a mile race in three minutes and 59.4 seconds.

1994 **The Channel Tunnel, or Chunnel, finally opens after years and years of digging.** The world's longest undersea tunnel connects England and France and involved boring machines starting in each country and meeting in the middle. Happily, both sides drilled to precisely the right spot and connected.

MAY 7

1867 **Dynamite is patented by Alfred Nobel.** While explosives were used in China centuries before, Nobel's innovations made the boom much bigger. His distress over dynamite being used as a weapon of war rather than an implement of mining may have been one of the reasons that he created the Nobel Peace Prize.

1915 A German U-boat torpedoes the British luxury steamship *Lusitania*, killing 1,195 people, including 123 Americans. At the time, the U.S. was neutral in World War I, but this tragedy ignited public outrage and eventually led to the U.S. joining the fight against Germany.

2015 Divers in Madagascar find what is believed to be part of the lost treasure of Captain Kidd the pirate. It's a solid silver bar that weighs 110 pounds.

MAY 8

1886 • Thirsty for some beverage trivia? On this day, Dr. John Stith Pemberton, a pharmacist in Atlanta, lets people sample his new syrup drink at Jacobs' Pharmacy. He adds carbonated water to it, charges 5 cents a glass, and Coca-Cola is born.

1945 • **The United States, Great Britain, and their allies celebrate Victory in Europe Day, known as VE Day, after Germany surrenders during World War II.**

1980 • The World Health Organization announces that smallpox has been eradicated. The terrible disease killed hundreds of millions of people before a vaccine wiped it off the face of the earth.

MAY 9

1886 • Firefighters in New Mexico rescue a bear cub from a raging wildfire. The cub, nicknamed Smokey, becomes the living icon of the U.S. Forest Service's Smokey Bear campaign, which began in 1944 with the slogan "Only you can prevent forest fires." After the real Smokey recovered from injuries from the fire, he was sent to live in the National Zoo in Washington, D.C. He was so popular and received so many letters that the U.S. Forest Service and the U.S. Postal Service gave Smokey his own zip code.

1945 • After studying a nest containing two-foot-long, 90-million-year-old eggs, **scientists announce they have discovered a new species, which they name *Beibeilong sinensis*, or "baby dragon from China."** Wait, dragons are real?!

MAY 10

It's National Clean Up Your Room Day!

We don't blame you if you want to pretend you didn't read this and just move on!

1869 To mark the completion of the transcontinental railroad, the presidents of the Union Pacific and Central Pacific railroads meet in Promontory, Utah, and drive a ceremonial last spike (the Golden Spike) into a rail line that connects their railroads. The spike was about six inches long, weighed 15.39 ounces and was made of 17.6-karat gold. The construction of the railway took seven years and involved thousands of Chinese laborers performing dangerous work to complete it.

1960 U.S. atomic submarine USS *Triton* returns home after completing the first fully submerged trip around the globe, staying underwater for almost 61 days and taking on fresh air every night from its snorkel. That crew was surely in desperate need of some fresh food when they pulled into port.

MAY 11

868 The earliest dated printed book—still in existence!—is created in ancient China. A Chinese translation of a Sanskrit text, *The Diamond Sutra* is a collection of seven woodblock prints glued together to create one long scroll that explains Buddhist teachings.

1904 **Spanish painter Salvador Dalí is born.** Dalí became super famous for his surrealist paintings, which were dreamlike images of weird and wonderful things. His most well-known work is called *The Persistence of Time,* which features melting clocks drooping all over a strange landscape.

1934 The combination of over-farming and a great storm in the U.S. prairies sends millions of tons of topsoil into the air and carries it away as far as New York. The Dust Bowl, as the period becomes known, was devastating, forcing out-of-work farmers to move to California and other areas in desperate search for jobs and fertile ground.

2000 A cute little baby named Astha Arora is born in India. What's so special about that? With her birth, India's population officially reaches 1 billion people. That was about 720 million more people than in the U.S. in a country about one third the size.

1881 • **The first electric streetcars start rolling out on city streets outside Berlin**, replacing horse-drawn trolleys. The cars were much faster than the horses and, we assume, pooped a lot less.

1968 • It's Tony Hawk's birthday. Hawk began skateboarding at the age of 9 and was one of the key figures who helped make freestyle skateboarding a global sensation.

MAY 13

1846 • Following President James K. Polk's request, Congress declares war on Mexico. And after two years of fighting the Mexican–American War (during which many future Civil War Union and Confederate generals fought side by side), the Rio Grande River was officially made the southern boundary of Texas; Arizona, California, Colorado, Nevada, New Mexico, and Utah were ceded to the United States.

1958 • **After 10 years, 11,050 miles, and 38 countries, adventurer Ben Carlin is the first and only person to travel around the world in an amphibious vehicle.** He dubbed his customized Jeep "Half-Safe." It was capable of chugging across oceans and driving over mountains...with a lot of stops for repairs. Did we mention the trip took 10 years to complete?

1995 • Alison Hargreaves is first woman climber to reach the summit of Mount Everest without an oxygen tank or any help from a climbing companion. (The air near the top of Mount Everest is so thin that the majority of climbers need oxygen tanks to survive.) The tank-less feat was first accomplished on May 8, 1978, by Reinhold Messner and Peter Habeler, who unlike soloist Hargreaves, helped each other accomplish the historic feat.

MAY 14

1607   •   Jamestown, the first permanent English settlement in North America, is established on the banks of the James River. The first two years were terrible—settlers faced famine and fighting with local indigenous people. But a time of peace and prosperity came after colonist John Rolfe married Pocahontas, the daughter of the Powhatan Confederacy's chief.

1948   •   Israel issues a Declaration of Independence in the middle of a civil war raging between the region's Jewish and Arab populations. That same day, President Harry S. Truman formally recognized Israel as a new nation.

2016   •   **Surfing pro Gabriel Medina** does the impossible: He lands the first-ever backflip in competitive surfing. "I can't believe my eyes!" said a nearby shark.

★ **It's Mother's Day!**

Moms are celebrated in North America every year on the second Sunday of May. You know what moms like even more than flowers and presents? Hugs!

MAY 15

1869   •   The National Woman Suffrage Association, dedicated to fighting for women's right to vote in America, is founded. Susan B. Anthony was the organization's first president. Quoting some of the words in the U.S. Constitution, she explained, "It was *we, the people*; not *we, the white male citizens*; nor yet *we, the male citizens*; but we, the whole people, who formed the Union."

1918   •   U.S. airmail service begins between Washington, D.C., Philadelphia, and New York City. Sure beats making a paper airplane out of your letter and flinging it out the window.

2008   •   **California Supreme Court rules in favor of same-sex marriage, granting LGBTQ couples the same rights as heterosexual couples.** Then in 2015, the U.S. Supreme Court ruled that the Constitution guarantees same-sex marriage rights for all Americans.

2010   •   You go girl—around the world! At the age of 16, fearless Jessica Watson becomes the youngest person to sail solo, nonstop and unassisted, around the globe.

2013   •   Scientists successfully clone stem cells, which can be developed into muscle, nerve, and other cells.

1888 — **Scientist Nikola Tesla lectures about his new alternating-current electric power system.** It is the system that we still use today, which is why Tesla is sometimes referred to as the man who invented the future.

1939 — The first Food Stamp program goes into effect, helping people who need assistance buy groceries and farmers sell surplus food. This program aided approximately 20 million people.

MAY 17

1875 — The first running of the Most Exciting Two minutes in Sports, a.k.a. the Kentucky Derby, is held. It's now the longest-running annual sports event in America and has been postponed only twice in its nearly 150-year history.

1900 — **The first printing of *The Wonderful Wizard of Oz* by author L. Frank Baum comes off the press.** There are a lot of differences between the book and the movie, like Dorothy's ruby red shoes. They are silver in the book, but the filmmakers thought red would look better against the yellow brick road.

HAS ANYONE SEEN MY SHOES? I CAN'T FIND THEM ANYWHERE!

1939 — The first televised game of baseball is broadcast on NBC, with Princeton defeating Columbia 2-1. Did they have instant replay? Uh, no. In fact, the first broadcast had only one camera that couldn't even show the entire field.

1954 — In the case of *Brown v. Board of Education*, the Supreme Court rules that separating children in public schools on the basis of their race is unconstitutional. The decision revolved around Linda Brown, a third-grade Black girl who wasn't allowed into her local school in Topeka, Kansas, because of the color of her skin.

MAY 18

1830 • British engineer Edwin Budding signs a contract to sell his invention: the lawnmower. Gee, thanks for the new chore, Budding!

1927 • **The grand opening of the world-famous Grauman's Chinese Theatre in Hollywood.** Why is this movie house, now named the TCL Chinese Theatre, world famous? The cement courtyard and sidewalk out front are lined with hand and foot imprints of superfamous stars. So, if you visit, you can measure your hand to see if it is bigger or smaller than those of different celebs. Think your hand is bigger than the Rock's?

1980 • Mount St. Helens, a volcano in Washington state, has a massive eruption that kills 57 people and devastates more than 200 square miles of surrounding wilderness.

MAY 19

1536 • Queen Anne Boleyn is beheaded so that Henry VIII can marry wife number three, Jane Seymour. Despite the horrific ending of her parents' marriage, Queen Elizabeth I, Henry and Anne's daughter, goes on to rule England for more than 40 years.

1643 • The United Colonies of New England is formed, formalizing a military coalition between Massachusetts Bay, Plymouth, Connecticut, and New Haven to support one another against attacks by Native Americans, the French, and the Dutch. While disagreements eventually break up the union, historians believe that the experience of working together inspired future colonies to join forces during the American Revolution.

1991 • **Race car driver Willy T. Ribbs becomes first Black driver to qualify to race in the Indianapolis 500.**

MAY 20

1862 President Abraham Lincoln signs the Homestead Act into law, which provides 160 acres of land to any adult U.S. citizen willing to go out and settle in the American West. The price of the land? It was $1.25 per acre if you stayed there for six months and made improvements. (In case you're wondering, that was ridiculously cheap even back then.)

873 Businessman Levi Strauss and tailor Jacob Davis button up their patent for one of the most famous garments ever: blue jeans. Try saying "pants patent" five times fast.

★ It's National Rescue Dog Day!

If there's one in your home, give 'em a belly rub for us!

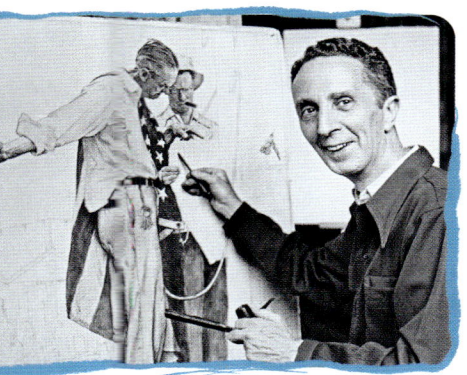

1916 **Artist Norman Rockwell, who was famous for capturing images of small-town America, paints his first cover for the *Saturday Evening Post*.** He painted 323 covers for the magazine over the course of his career.

2015 Adele's album *25* sells a record-breaking 3.38 million copies in its first week in the United States. Is it weird that a *great record* is a *broken record*?

2020 The most delicious accident ever: A truck overturns on an interstate in Nashville, spilling 40,000 pounds of mac and cheese all over the road.

MAY 21

1881 Humanitarian Clara Barton founds the American National Red Cross, an organization dedicated to giving food, shelter, and medical aid to victims of wars and natural disasters.

1904 FIFA officially forms with the goal of making everyone in the world fans of soccer goals.

1927 Thirty-three and a half hours after taking off from Long Island, New York, aviator Charles Lindbergh lands his plane, *The Spirit of St Louis*, outside Paris, making him the first person to fly solo across the Atlantic Ocean.

1932 **Aviator Amelia Earhart becomes the second person and first woman to fly solo across the Atlantic after flying 17 hours from Newfoundland to Northern Ireland.** In 1937, while attempting to become the first female pilot to fly completely around the world, she went missing over the Pacific and was never seen again.

MAY 22

1842 — **The first major wagon train sets off on the Oregon Trail**, a 2,000-mile route from Missouri to Oregon, which was eventually used by hundreds of thousands of pioneers moving out west.

1960 — The largest earthquake ever recorded—a magnitude 9.5—hits Chile. Called Valdivia after the city it nearly completely destroyed, the earthquake triggered a massive tsunami that caused tremendous damage to towns all the way across the Pacific Ocean on the shores of New Zealand, Japan, the Philippines, and Hawaii.

1980 — The first Pac-Man arcade game is installed in a movie theater in Tokyo. It became one of the most popular video games ever, even inspiring the hit song "Pac-Man Fever" about the craze.

MAY 23

1785 — **Benjamin Franklin announces his invention of bifocals**, glasses with lenses that help people see things up close and also far away.

1934 — Criminals Clyde Champion Barrow and Bonnie Elizabeth Parker, better known as Bonnie and Clyde, are finally stopped and killed by officers after a two-year bank-robbing crime spree that made them famous and feared throughout America.

1962 — In an amazing advancement in medical science, surgeons in Boston successfully reattach the arm of a boy named Everett "Red" Knowles. Red had lost his arm while jumping up and grabbing on to a moving train. Postsurgery, he regained full use of his arm, which he hopefully used to hold only train tickets and not trains anymore.

1883 • **The Brooklyn Bridge opens, connecting Brooklyn and Manhattan over the East River.** At the time, it was the largest suspension bridge in the world. More than 14,000 miles of wire were used to make up its signature web of cables.

1895 • **Henry Irving becomes the first actor to receive a knighthood from the Queen of England.** Since then, many prominent people have been knighted Dame or Sir, including Julie Andrews (the star of the original *Mary Poppins*) and Michael Caine (who played Alfred in *Batman Begins*).

How Do You Get Knighted?

Since Henry Irving, lots of celebrities, artists, and sports figures have been knighted. How do you become a Sir or a Dame? Just do something that the royal family thinks is supercool. (Pro tip: If you don't want to lose your ears, try not to move around too much as King Charles taps each of your shoulders with the flat part of a giant sword.)

MAY 25

1787 • Well, we won independence, maybe we should make some laws? On this day 55 state delegates, including George Washington, James Madison, and Benjamin Franklin, head to Philadelphia to begin composing the U.S. Constitution.

2001 • Adventurer Erik Weihenmayer is the first blind person to climb to the summit of Mount Everest. Weihenmayer has dedicated his life to inspiring others to chase their dreams. "I think this is the best time in history, the most precious time in history to be a pioneer, to reach out, to seize hold of adversity and challenges we face, to harness energy not only to transform our own lives but to elevate the world around us."

2020 • George Floyd, a Black man, is murdered while being pinned to the ground by Minneapolis police during an arrest. A bystander's video of the event later ignites nationwide protests against racism and police brutality in more than 100 cities around the country. The officer who pressed his knee into Floyd's neck was convicted of second- and third-degree murder, as well as manslaughter, and sentenced to 22 and a half years in prison. Three other officers involved in the tragedy were also sentenced to time in prison.

MAY 26

1923 — This sounds safe, right? **The inaugural 24 Hours of Le Mans endurance race gets going.** Two-person driver teams race around Le Mans, France, for 24 hours straight. The first ones to cross the finish line a day after the race started were André Lagache and René Léonard, who surely celebrated with a really long nap.

1940 — The evacuation of Dunkirk begins. This famous mission during World War II rescued 338,226 allied troops who were trapped in France. They used more than 800 vessels, including massive Royal Navy destroyers and the small fishing boats of civilians who volunteered and risked their lives to save the troops.

2002 — Eminem releases his fourth studio album, *The Eminem Show*, which becomes the best-selling hip-hop record of all time. At last count, it sold more than 27 million copies. (That must have taken a long time to count!)

★ It's National Paper Airplane Day!

To make the perfect aerodynamic craft, follow these directions from *Popular Mechanics*.

1 Draw this airplane shape in the middle of a sheet of paper.

2 Fold the paper in half down the center of the plane. Cut along the perimeter to get a perfectly symmetrical aircraft.

3 First, fold the wings down along line No. 1. Then grab the tail at the center and fold it in the opposite direction along the same line so it extends about the wings. Next, fold down along line No 2.

4 At the seams where the wings meet, use a piece of Scotch tape to hold them together.

5 Add a standard paper clip beside the nose to balance the weight of the thinner nose with the plane's wide wings. Last, fold the flaps up along line No. 3.

6 After the test flight, troubleshoot by adjusting those folds. If the plane nosedives, bend the rear flap to make them more vertical. If it swoops up and then dives straight down, flatten them.

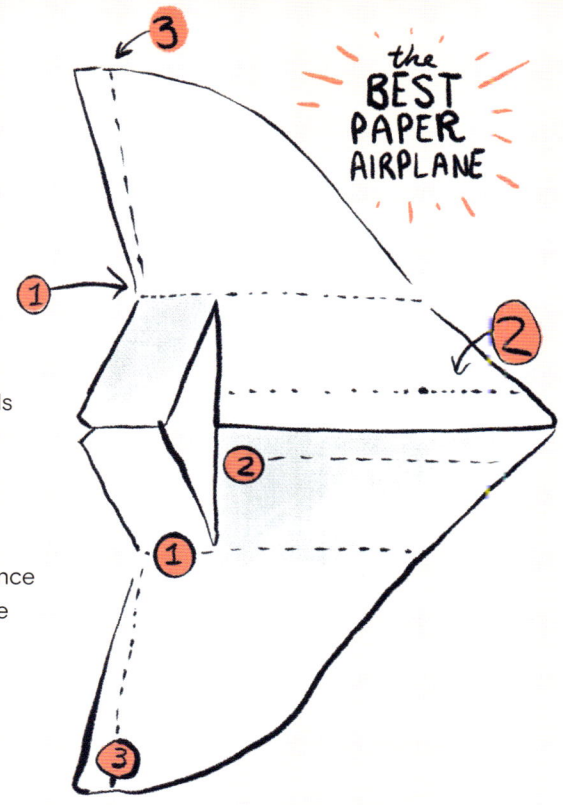

the BEST PAPER AIRPLANE

MAY **27**

1837 — It's the birthday of Wild Bill Hickok, a real American frontiersman, whose gunfighting skills became the stuff of legend. Wild Bill was said to have battled (and won) many a Wild West shootout and once killed an angry bear with a knife.

1933 — Cartoonist and world traveler Robert Ripley opens his first Odditorium at the 1933 World's Fair. The attraction features strange items and interesting people he featured in his popular "Believe It or Not" cartoons, like Alvarez Kanichka, who freaked out audiences by swallowing plugged in electric light bulbs, and Harry McGregor, who would pull his wife on a wagon using a hook attached to his eyelids. Ouch!

2018 — South Korean boy band BTS make history as the first K-pop group to have a number one hit on the *Billboard* 200 with their album *Love Yourself Tear*. Going on hiatus in 2022, the band members prepared to start their required military service in the South Korean army, with Jin being the first to do so.

2022 — **The fourth season of *Stranger Things* is released on Netflix, featuring the role-playing game Dungeons & Dragons.** D&D (as most people refer to it) was originally released in 1974 and was a cultural phenomenon in the 1980s.

MAY **28**

1742 — The first indoor swimming pool in Britain, called the Bagnio, opens in Goodman's Fields, London. The first belly flop soon followed.

1830 — President Andrew Jackson signs the Indian Removal Act, which forces Cherokee, Chickasaw, Choctaw, Creek, and Seminole tribes out of Georgia and surrounding states. After resisting, thousands of Cherokee are led out at gunpoint in a tragic and deadly march known as the Trail of Tears.

1961 — British lawyer Peter Benenson publishes an article called "The Forgotten Prisoners," calling for the release of all people who were imprisoned because they peacefully expressed their political or religious beliefs. The article leads to a movement that eventually becomes Amnesty International, a nonpolitical group that fights for human rights around the world.

MAY 29

1953 — **Mountain climbers Edmund Hillary of New Zealand and Tenzing Norgay of Nepal become the first people to reach the highest point on earth, the summit of Mount Everest.** They were not the first to try, however. One climber named George Leigh Mallory, who made several failed attempts, was asked by a journalist why he wanted to climb the mountain. His answer is one of the most famous three-word phrases ever uttered: "Because it's there."

1999 — Even higher up than Mount Everest? The International Space Station. On this day, the *Discovery* performed the first space shuttle docking with the station.

MAY 30

1868 — The first Memorial Day is observed at Arlington Cemetery in Washington, D.C., honoring the soldiers of the North and the South who died fighting the Civil War. In 1971, the official holiday, which had been extended to honor those who died in any of America's conflicts, was shifted to the last Monday of May.

1911 — **The first Indianapolis 500 speeds off, with racer Ray Harroun coming in first with an average speed of 74.602 mph.** The Indy 500 is one of the most well-known races in the world with one of the oddest traditions: The winner usually drinks a bottle of buttermilk in Victory Lane.

1943 — The All-American Girls Professional Baseball League steps up to bat. The league was established by Philip K. Wrigley, who was looking for a way to keep professional baseball parks open. All-male minor league teams had been shutting down because players were being drafted during World War II. The women's league was a hit and operated from 1943 to 1954.

MAY 31

1921 — In a horrible incident of violent racism, thousands of white citizens in Tulsa, Oklahoma, storm the mostly Black Greenwood neighborhood. The rioters burned down homes and businesses in the prosperous district known as Black Wall Street and killed hundreds of people. The terrible day came to be known as the Tulsa Race Massacre, and for many years, news organizations and politicians conspired to cover it up and pretended it never happened.

THIS DAY IN *my* HISTORY
MAY

Fill in any memorable events from your life here.

1 ....

2 ....

3 ....

4 ....

5 ....

6 ....

7 ....

8 ....

9 ....

10 ....

11 ....

12 ....

13 ....

14 ....

15 ....

16 ....

17 ....

18 ....

19 ....

20 ....

21 ....

22 ....

23 ....

24 ....

25 ....

26 ....

27 ....

28 ....

29 ....

30 ....

31 ....

JUNE 1

I**T'S LGBTQ PRIDE MONTH!** All around the world, parades, speeches, and events recognize the positive impact that lesbian, gay, bisexual, and transgender individuals have had on history and will have in the future.

1831 • British explorer Sir James Clark Ross locates the Magnetic North Pole. Wait, what's that? Well, the Geographic (True) North Pole is the spot at the top of the globe where all of the lines of longitude meet, and it is the north axis of the line that the earth rotates on. The Magnetic North Pole is the spot where the lines of force of the earth's magnetic field converge. It is actually several hundred miles away from the actual North Pole, and here's the weird part: it's always moving.

1988 • **Madden Football—which becomes the best-selling sports video game year after year—is released.** NFL coach and broadcasting legend John Madden admitted that he didn't know much about computers or gaming, but he insisted to developers that the game with his name on it would be authentic to real game play and serve as a teaching tool for future players and coaches.

JUNE 2

1835 • P.T. Barnum and his circus begin their first tour of the United States. Barnum is remembered as "the greatest showman on earth." His museum and circus delighted (and sometimes) fooled audience members with exhibits like **"the Feejee Mermaid," which had the body of a monkey and the tail of a fish.** Freaky!

1953 • Queen Elizabeth II is officially crowned the Queen of England at age 25 (even though she took on the role in 1952 immediately following her father's death). She went on to become the subject of countless movies, TV shows, and books and has the second-longest royal reign in history—70 years and 214 days. (French King Louis XIV holds the record, with a reign of 72 years, but he got a head start on Queen Elizabeth: He was only 4 years old when he took the throne.)

1969 • **One of the most famous kids' books (that we bet has a spot on your bookshelf) crawls into existence: *The Very Hungry Caterpillar* by Eric Carle.**

2010 • Six volunteers step inside an isolated chamber where they will live for the next 520 days to simulate a Mars mission. They could only speak with friends and family through a purposely very slow computer system, and the crew ate only the same foods served on the International Space Station. Lots and lots of freeze-dried stuff. (Did we mention they volunteered to do this and weren't being punished?)

2017 • Rock climber Alex Honnold makes the first free solo ascent of El Capitan in Yosemite National Park. He climbed the 2,900-foot route with no assistance and no safety ropes.

JUNE **4**

1783 • **Brothers Joseph and Étienne Montgolfier give the first public demonstration of their new invention: the hot-air balloon.** They sent it up without any passengers, then a few months later they sent another balloon up with a sheep, a rooster, and a duck as test pilots. Guess the brothers should also get credit for inventing the first flying farm?

1940 • British Prime Minister Winston Churchill delivers one of history's most famous speeches, bolstering his county's courage against the Nazis. He says, in part, "[W]e shall defend our Island, whatever the cost may be, we shall fight on the beaches, we shall fight on the landing grounds, we shall fight in the fields and in the streets, we shall fight in the hills; we shall never surrender..."

1991 • You never know when you'll turn into an accidental treasure hunter. A guy bought an old painting at a flea market in Pennsylvania for $4 because he liked the frame. After he got it home, he opened the back of the painting and found a folded-up document. It turned out to be an official copy of the Declaration of Independence made in 1776. On this day in 1991, the $4 find is auctioned at Sotheby's and sells for $2.42 million!

JUNE 5

1947 • At Harvard's graduation ceremony, U.S. Secretary of State George C. Marshall gives a speech outlining the Marshall Plan, a program to rebuild and restabilize post-World War II Europe that would be paid for by the United States. We're sure the graduates were, like, "Wait, isn't this speech supposed to be about us?"

1967 • The Six-Day War—in which Israel fights Egypt, Syria, and Jordan—begins. Israel seized a significant amount of land in the bloody conflict before the U.N. brokered a cease-fire.

JUNE 6

1896 • Two fishermen, George Harbo and Frank Samuelson, get in a rowboat in New York City and don't stop rowing until they reach France 55 days later, making them the first to row across the Atlantic. They hoped their journey would make them fabulously rich, but mostly it just made them really tired.

1933 • **The first drive-in movie theater opens.** At one point, there were more than 4,000 of them spread across America. It was a fun new way to take in a flick—plus there was never any problem finding a parking spot.

1944 • Operation Overlord begins with the D-Day invasions, as Allied forces land in Normandy, France, during World War II. It was the largest invasion in history, involving 7,000 ships manned by more than 195,000 naval personnel from eight countries. Almost 133,000 troops from England, Canada, and the United States landed during this bloody and ultimately successful attack.

JUNE 7

1968 • **The first LEGOLAND in the world opens in Denmark.** The place is decorated with models of famous landmarks and cityscapes that required more than 20 million bricks to build. That instruction booklet must have been huge!

❓ Did You Know?

Vikings are usually depicted wearing helmets with horns on them, but there is no physical evidence that they actually did this in real life.

> IT JUST FEELS LIKE SOMETHING IS MISSING...

452

The Huns, a nomadic tribe from Central Asia, invade Italy, led by the feared Attila the Hun. Attila was a ruthless leader who is believed to have grabbed power by murdering his own brother. Under his rule, the Huns greatly expanded their empire, as Attila won nearly every battle he fought. The Romans called him the Scourge of God, because he brutally sacked and pillaged Roman cities again and again.

793

An attack on a small community in Northumbria (which is now made up of northern England and southeast Scotland) brings about the Viking Age of Conquest. For three centuries, the Vikings used their expertise at sea to raid coastal villages and monasteries, attack trade ships, and plant their flag all over Britain the European continent as well as Russia, Iceland, Greenland, and Newfoundland.

JUNE **9**

1934

Donald Duck—the most famous cartoon waterbird in history (apologies to Daffy)—makes his first appearance in "The Wise Little Hen."

1973

Legendary thoroughbred Secretariat becomes the first horse in 25 years to win the Triple Crown, meaning he came in first place at the Kentucky Derby, the Preakness, and the Belmont Stakes. Secretariat wasn't the first horse to do it, but his win at the Belmont Stakes, where he finished 31 lengths ahead of his nearest competitor, has been called the most amazing horse race of all time.

JUNE 10

1652 — In Boston, John Hull is commissioned to run the first mint in America. A mint is where they make money, and at that time, it was silver coins. Lucky for John, he got to keep 6 percent of all the silver he minted. Long story short, he became extremely wealthy.

1752 — **Inventor and future politician Benjamin Franklin flies a kite during a thunderstorm to prove that lightning is electricity.** That's how the story is commonly told anyway. Historians aren't exactly sure if he carried out the experiment or if it was just an idea he wrote down. Either way, do not try this at home!

1845 — We've heard of pets chewing up things or making a mess, but this is next-level misbehavior: At the funeral of President Andrew Jackson, his pet parrot, Poll, is removed from the services for swearing!

JUNE 11

1963 — After President Kennedy sends National Guard troops to the University of Alabama in Tuscaloosa, segregationist Alabama Governor George Wallace is forced to end a blockade and allow Black students to enroll.

2002 — *American Idol*, featuring judges Simon Cowell, Paula Abdul, and Randy Jackson, and a cavalcade of amazing (and amazingly bad) singers, premieres on Fox.

2009 — The World Health Organization declares the swine flu a global pandemic. It was called the swine flu because the virus is similar to one that harms pigs. Today this flu strain is under control but not eradicated.

JUNE 12

1817 — **German inventor Baron Karl von Drais rolls out the world's first bicycle.** It's made of wood and has no pedals, gears, or chains. Going downhill is a blast. Going uphill? Not so much.

1942 — On her 13th birthday, Anne Frank gets a diary for a present. Three weeks later, her family went into hiding from the Nazis, and she used the diary to document her life during this dark time in history. Her diary, which was later published as a book and has since sold more than 30 million copies, has become a symbol of bravery and resilience. In it, Frank wrote, "Where there's hope, there's life. It fills us with fresh courage and makes us strong again."

1922 A man named Charlie Osborne has an accident with a 350-pound hog—but that's not the weird part. After the incident, Osbourne caught a bad case of hiccups that lasted for 68 years! He holds the Guinness World Record for having the longest continuous hiccups—a record that no one wants to beat.

2000 **For the first time in five decades, leaders of North and South Korea come together for a summit meeting.** The two countries were technically still at war—and still are today—since the Korean War ended with a cease-fire and not a treaty. Soldiers on each side guard the border and monitor the other side for signs of hostility.

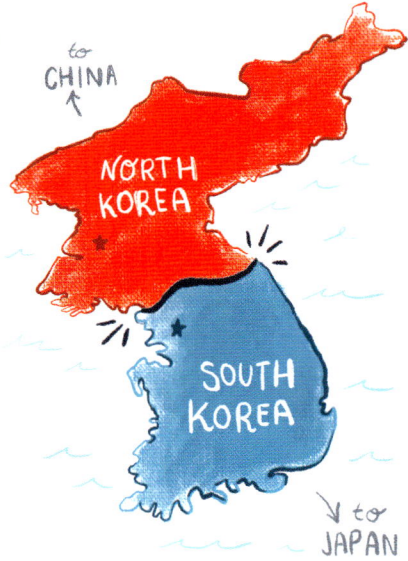

2010 Paul the Octopus correctly predicts the outcome of the first of many World Cup matches. How did he make his predictions? Two boxes filled with his favorite food, mussels, were labeled with opposing teams' flags and lowered into his tank. Whichever box he started snacking on was his pick. Paul snacked correctly eight times in a row! Then he apparently got too full and retired from the betting business a couple days after the World Cup Final.

JUNE 14

1777 During the American Revolution, **the Continental Congress announces that "the flag of the thirteen United States be thirteen stripes alternate red and white," and that "the Union be thirteen stars, white on a blue field, representing a new Constellation."** While there's no real documentation for this moment, the accepted history is that George Washington personally asked Philadelphia seamstress Betsy Ross to stitch together the first Stars and Stripes.

2009 NBA coach Phil Jackson wins a record-setting 10th NBA championship when the Los Angeles Lakers beat the Orlando Magic. By the time he retired, he had 13 rings—11 earned as a coach; two as a player.

JUNE 15

1878

People used to argue as to whether a horse's feet all left the ground while galloping. On June 15, photographer Eadweard Muybridge gave them an answer: yes. **Muybridge used high-speed photography to capture a horse in motion frame by frame,** not only settling the debate, but also revolutionizing photography.

★ It's National Megalodon Day!

Why would a shark get an annual celebration? Well, this prehistoric fish was very, very big and likely weighed as much as 30 great white sharks combined. You want to be the one to tell it that it doesn't get its own special day?

JUNE 16

1884

The first roller coaster in America opens at Coney Island. It wasn't exactly what we know as roller coasters today. It zipped along at a hair-raising...6 mph. By comparison, the fastest roller coaster in the world right now, the Formula Rossa, reaches speeds of 149 mph. Still, 6 mph is more fun than walking, right?

CAN THIS THING GO ANY FASTER?

1963

Soviet cosmonaut Valentina Tereshkova takes off on board *Vostok 6* and becomes the first woman in space. Tereshkova orbited earth 48 times before returning home. Wow, we get dizzy just reading that.

What Are the Seven Man-Made Wonders of the World?

1 THE CHICHEN ITZA

A Mayan holy site in Mexico featuring a temple that has 365 steps—one for each day of the year.

2 CHRIST THE REDEEMER

A 98-foot-tall statue of Jesus Christ at the summit of Mount Corcovado in Brazil, completed in 1931.

3 THE COLOSSEUM

An ancient Roman gladiator arena in Italy built in 72 CE.

4 GREAT WALL OF CHINA

A 13,000-mile wall constructed over the course of more than 2,000 years.

5 MACHU PICCHU

A 15th-century Incan royal estate built atop the Andes Mountains that stretches over five miles.

6 PETRA

Dating around 300 BCE, a city in Jordan carved into pink sandstone cliffs, nicknamed the "Rose City."

7 TAJ MAHAL

An ivory marble mausoleum in India.

1632 ● **Construction of the enormous Taj Mahal begins.** This 42-acre building and garden complex was commissioned by emperor Shah Jahan as a resting place for his beloved departed wife, Mumtaz Mahal. Finishing the Taj Mahal required more than 20,000 workers and 1,000 elephants and took 20 years to complete.

1885 ● The Statue of Liberty arrives in New York Harbor after being shipped across the Atlantic Ocean from France in 350 pieces. A year later, the reassembled copper-and-iron statue was officially unveiled as a symbol of freedom, democracy, and the welcoming possibilities of life in America.

JUNE 18

1812 — The War of 1812 begins between the U.S. and Great Britain. At one point, British troops ransacked Washington, D.C., and set the White House on fire. America was able to turn the tide, however, and prevailed. During one notable victory at Baltimore's Fort McHenry, U.S. troops flew a huge American flag to celebrate, and the sight inspired Francis Scott Key to write what eventually became our national anthem.

1815 — The war- and territory-hungry French military leader (and sometimes emperor) Napoleon Bonaparte is decisively defeated at the Battle of Waterloo, where the men of an estimated 40,000 French troops were either captured, wounded, or killed by the opposing British forces led by the Duke of Wellington. Today, the expression meet your Waterloo basically means you got your butt totally kicked.

1983 — **Astronaut Sally Ride takes a ride aboard the space shuttle *Challenger*, becoming the first American woman in space.**

JUNE 19

1865 — Juneteenth, which is short for June Nineteenth, marks the day when **Union General Gordon Granger arrived in Texas to inform the enslaved people there that Confederate General Robert E. Lee had surrendered two months earlier, and they were now free.** Juneteenth became a federal holiday on June 17, 2021.

1910 — The first Father's Day is celebrated in Spokane, Washington.

1978 — The most famous grumpy cat in the world, Garfield, makes his first comic strip appearance in more than 40 American newspapers.

JUNETEENTH

1840 • American inventor Samuel F.B. Morse gets a U.S. patent for Morse code, a telegraph communication system using dots and dashes.

Use the Morse code alphabet to secretly "say" anything by simply tapping any surface.

A dot (.) is a quick tap; a dash (–) is a little longer:

A .-	G --.	M --	S ...	Y -.--	4 ....-
B -...	H	N -.	T -	Z --..	5 .....
C -.-.	I ..	O ---	U ..-	0 -----	6 -....
D -..	J .---	P .--.	V ...-	1 .----	7 --...
E .	K -.-	Q --.-	W .--	2 ..---	8 ---..
F ..-.	L .-..	R .-.	X -..-	3 ...--	9 ----.

One of the most famous, and useful if you need help, Morse code messages is S.O.S., which stands for *Save Our Souls*:

S.O.S. ... --- ...

1975 • The movie *Jaws*, directed by Steven Spielberg, about a great white shark terrorizing a beach community, is released. It was a megahit and created the concept of the summer blockbuster, which continues today. (As do *Jaws*-induced nightmares about becoming a shark snack!)

2005 • **Artist chimpanzee Congo has three of his colorful abstract paintings auctioned off.** How much would you pay for a chimp-made picture? A California man named Howard Hong paid $25,000. That's a lot of bananas!

JUNE 21

1893 • Ready for a wheel-y good time? **George Washington Gale Ferris Jr., a 34-year-old engineer from Pittsburgh, opens his new invention, the Ferris Wheel, at the World Columbian Exposition in Chicago.**

1982 • Failed assassin John W. Hinckley, Jr., who shot President Ronald Reagan and three others in Washington, D.C., was found not guilty of attempted murder by reason of insanity.

2005 • A massive communication outage that stopped phone and Internet service and shut down air travel and the stock exchange in New Zealand was caused by rats chewing through a massive fiber optic cable on the east side of North Island, and coincidentally, also by a human worker who accidentally cut a fiber optic cable on the west side. Were they in cahoots?

★ It's the Summer Solstice!

Due to the earth's tilt, this the longest day of the year in the Northern Hemisphere. It usually falls on the 20th, 21st, or 22nd, and is astronomically the first day of summer. Depending where you live, you might not see sunset until 9 o'clock at night.

JUNE 22

1934 • **Bank robber and escaped felon John Dillinger is named America's first public enemy number one on his 31st birthday.** The federal government offered a $10,000 reward for his capture and a $5,000 reward for information leading to his arrest. Dillinger was betrayed by a friend, Anna Sage, who told agents about his planned trip to see a movie. Walking out of the theater on July 22, 1934, Dillinger was ambushed and killed by authorities. Despite being wanted for multiple violent crimes, Dillinger had become a folk hero to angry people who had lost their money in failed banks.

1944 • President Franklin D. Roosevelt signs the G.I. Bill, which gives veterans returning from World War II help with medical, housing, and educational expenses as a thank you for their service.

1281 Mongolian ships, under the command of Kublai Khan, set sail from Korea to invade Japan, but weeks later the ships are destroyed by a typhoon that the Japanese named Kamikaze (meaning *divine winds*).

1961 The Antarctic Treaty bans any military activity on the continent, designating it as a place of international research and cooperation.

2014 **Astronomers reveal the discovery of a white dwarf star that has become so cool that its carbon has crystallized into an earth-size diamond.** Want to go get it? It's going to be a very long trip. This big diamond is several trillion miles away.

2016 The United Kingdom votes to leave the European Union in a controversial referendum called Brexit (which is a combination of British and exit).

JUNE 24

1901 **The first major exhibition by artist Pablo Picasso, who is 19, opens in Paris.**

2010 The longest match in tennis history finally ends with American John Isner defeating French player Nicolas Mahut at Wimbledon. The match lasted more than 11 hours and stretched out over three days because Wimbledon didn't have lights, and it kept getting too dark to see the ball.

Who Was Pablo Picasso?

Pablo Picasso was a Spanish artist who, along with Georges Braque, created a style of artwork called cubism. Cubism is an abstract style of painting that shows objects or people from multiple angles all at once and uses geometric shapes like cubes, triangles, and cones to represent "normal" features on a person's face. One of Picasso's most famous works is *Guernica*, a 25-foot-wide painting depicting the tragedy of war. Want to try your hand at cubism? Draw your face like it is made up of puzzle pieces, then shift the puzzle pieces around. Who says both of your eyes can't be on one side of your nose?

JUNE 25

1776 The first $2 bills are issued, making them nine days older than America. They are still printed, but the reason you don't see them a lot is because people think they are collectors' items and don't spend them. Are they really worth something? Yes, two dollars.

1867 Ouch! Inventor Lucien B. Smith applies for one of the first patents for barbed wire.

1876 The Battle of the Little Bighorn is fought between Federal troops led by Lieutenant Colonel George Armstrong Custer and Lakota Sioux and Cheyenne warriors led by Sitting Bull. The Federal troops lose in the battle that became known as Custer's Last Stand.

1929 President Herbert Hoover authorizes the construction of the massive Hoover Dam. At its base, the dam is wider than two football fields, and when it was finished, it was the world's largest hydroelectric station, producing power for Nevada, Arizona, and California.

1978 In San Francisco, a rainbow flag is used in a gay pride march for the first time and becomes a symbol for the LGBTQ community.

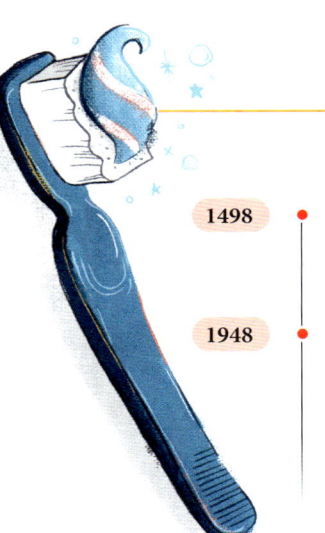

JUNE 26

1498 Smile! The emperor of China patents the bristle toothbrush. Before his invention, people used frayed wood sticks to brush their teeth (and probably gave themselves a lot of splinters in their gums).

1948 The Berlin Airlift commences. At the end of World War II, Germany was divided into areas controlled by America, Great Britain, France, and the Soviet Union. But Soviet leader Josef Stalin attempted to grab total control, ordering a blockade of supplies to people living in the western half of the capital city Berlin. President Harry Truman responded with an operation that delivered 2.3 million tons of food, clothing, water, medicine, and fuel to trapped Berliners.

1974 A pack of Wrigley's chewing gum is the first-ever item scanned at a supermarket checkout with a UPC (Universal Product Code).

1997 *Harry Potter and the Philosopher's Stone* by J.K. Rowling is released in British bookstores. Muggles go absolutely crazy for it, along with its eventual sequels, movies, and theme parks. Did you know that the book almost had a different title in America? Before changing *Philosopher's Stone* to *Sorcerer's Stone* for the U.S. edition, it was almost called *Harry Potter and the School of Magic*.

1950 — The United States officially enters the Korean War. After World War II, the Korean Peninsula was divided in half along the 38th parallel (or line of latitude), with the Soviet Union troops occupying the North and the U.S. troops occupying the South. When the Soviet-backed North army poured across the border, a war ensued. It lasted three years with millions injured or killed and resulted in no change in the nations' borders.

1957 — **The world's first ATM begins operation in London.** Before that, people had to scramble to get to the bank before it closed at 3:30 p.m. to take out cash. This innovation is great for last-minute pizza cravings—and not so great for money savings.

JUNE **28**

1914 — The assassination of Austrian Archduke Franz Ferdinand and his wife, Sophie, by Gavrilo Princip, a Bosnian Serb member of the secret society known as the Black Hand, sets off a chain of events that causes World War I.

1919 — Exactly five years after the assassination that started World War I, the Treaty of Versailles is signed, which outlines terms for peace. It took another five months before the armies laid down their weapons, ending the war that left 20 million dead and 21 million wounded.

1969 — After an early morning police raid of gay club the Stonewall Inn in New York City's Greenwich Village, a riot breaks out among patrons and locals who are fed up with harassment from the authorities. The riot led to six days of protest and became a defining moment for the gay-rights movement in America and around the world.

2009 — **Physicist Stephen Hawking throws a party for time travelers.** Wait, what? The genius scientist threw the party and then sent out invitations to it the next day. His theory was that if time travel was possible, someone from the future would see the invitation and go back in time to attend his event. Unfortunately, no one showed up, proving either that there is no such thing as time travel or that time travelers from the future are party poopers.

JUNE 29

1613 — The original Globe theater in London—where Shakespeare's plays were performed—burns down after a stage cannon sent a spark to the roof during a performance of *Henry VIII*. "Wherefore art thou, fire extinguisher?"

1995 — After the American space shuttle *Atlantis* docks with the Russian space station Mir, NASA calls it "a new era of friendship and cooperation" between two countries that battled for domination in space (not to mention land). The U.S. astronauts brought gifts of fruit, flowers, and chocolate. What's a zero-gravity sugar rush like?

JUNE 30

1520 — **After conquering Mexico, Spanish conquistador Hernán Cortés and his troops face an Aztec revolt.** The event came to be known as La Noche Triste (the Night of Sadness) by the Spanish. Many of Cortés's soldiers attempting to retreat drowned in Lake Texcoco when the vessel carrying them and their stolen Aztec treasures sank. Montezuma II, the last Aztec emperor, was killed during the struggle.

1937 — The world's first emergency call telephone service is launched in London using the number 999. The U.S. followed with 911 in 1968.

1985 — It's the birthday of swimming superstar Michael Phelps, the most decorated athlete in Olympic history. Phelps earned 28 medals altogether—winning eight gold medals during the 2008 games alone. Yeah, but can he do a good cannonball?

What Is the Legend of Montezuma's Cursed Treasure?

The treasure that was sunk (or thrown overboard by Spanish sailors hoping to lighten their load as they escaped) has never been recovered. A common belief is that the Aztecs found it and hid it in a secret location, possibly in what is now the United States. But while it is worth billions of dollars today, you probably don't want to go searching for it. Legend has it that the Aztecs cursed the treasure before burying it.

THIS DAY IN HISTORY
JUNE

Fill in any memorable events from your life here.

1 ....

2 ....

3 ....

4 ....

5 ....

6 ....

7 ....

8 ....

9 ....

10 ....

11 ....

12 ....

13 ....

14 ....

15 ....

16 ....

17 ....

18 ....

19 ....

20 ....

21 ....

22 ....

23 ....

24 ....

25 ....

26 ....

27 ....

28 ....

29 ....

30 ....

JULY 1

T'S DISABILITY PRIDE MONTH! Ever since the Americans with Disabilities Act passed in July of 1990, this month has been dedicated to celebrating people who do amazing things without letting physical or mental challenges get in their way.

1916 **The Battle of the Somme begins** to rage as Allied forces along the Western Front confront German forces near the Somme River in France. Lasting nearly five months, it became one of the most deadly, brutal battles in military history, with more than 1 million soldiers killed or wounded.

1941 The first TV commercial ever airs before a Brooklyn Dodgers game. It's an ad for the Bulova Watch Company, which features its slogan "America runs on Bulova time." (Wait, doesn't it run on Dunkin'?) Anyway, Bulova pays a $9 fee to run the ad. No, there are no zeros missing in that number: It cost only $9! Compare that to a 30-second-long commercial run during the Super Bowl these days, which can cost more than $6 million. Bargain of the century!

1997 Hong Kong, which was on a 99-year lease to Great Britain, is handed back to China. The ceremony was mostly peaceful, but more recently, numerous protests have sprung up in Hong Kong, led by pro-Democracy citizens who reject China's authoritarian rule.

JULY 2

1839 • Captured in Sierra Leone and placed on the Spanish schooner *La Amistad* heading for Cuba, Joseph Cinqué leads 52 of his fellow enslaved people to revolt and take over the ship. The ship was discovered off the coast of New York and the captives were imprisoned. Their plight soon became a news story that showed the horrors of slavery. Their case went all the way to the Supreme Court, where it was ruled that the prisoners were illegally kidnapped and should go free.

1964 • U.S. President Lyndon B. Johnson signs the Civil Rights Act into law. This landmark legislation makes it illegal for most businesses and organizations to discriminate against people based on their race, color, religion, gender, or national origin.

2018 • British divers John Volanthen and Richard Stanton finally reach a group of 12 boys and their soccer coach who are trapped inside the Laung cave complex in Thailand. Nine days before, the soccer team had been exploring in the caves when a huge rainstorm flooded all exits. Hundreds of rescuers from around the world teamed up to help locate the boys. After they were found, it took another eight days to get them out of the dangerous rocky network of pitch-black underwater tunnels.

JULY 3

1863 • The Civil War's Battle of Gettysburg, the largest battle ever fought on American soil, ends after three days of bloody combat. The Union prevailed, crushing Robert E. Lee's plans to invade the North and forcing a cease-fire.

2004 • **Magician Monty Witt organizes the longest linking-ring chain trick** with the help of 129 magicians, using 534 rings. Their feat lands them in the *Guinness Book of World Records*. Do you have 535 rings and 130 magician friends? If so, you can make their record disappear!

Little-Known Facts About This Historic Battle

1 A few female soldiers fought on both sides at Gettysburg.

2 The wagon train of wounded Confederates leaving the battlefield was 17 miles long.

3 Amazingly, 148 years after the battle was fought, caretakers of the Gettysburg National Military Park found two bullets from the battle embedded in an oak tree. Historians call that a Witness Tree because it was alive during the fight.

JULY 4

1776 **The signing of the Declaration of Independence happens**...*sort of.* July 4 is recognized as the official day that the 13 colonies demanded freedom from King George III and British rule, but the truth is that it took several months for the document to get signed by everyone. Some of the 56 signers weren't in Philadelphia where the Declaration had been penned, and there were no FedEx overnight options in colonial times.

The American Revolutionary War had started in 1775—before the Declaration was written—and lasted until 1783. Despite all those terrible years of battle, England is now one of America's greatest allies. (Another big difference between today and 1776? Neither country's leaders walk around in powdered wigs.)

1826 Sometimes friends and often brutal political enemies, founding fathers Thomas Jefferson and John Adams die on the same exact day just hours apart. Adams was 90 years old, Jefferson was 83.

1997 *Mars Pathfinder* successfully parachutes onto Mars and starts rolling and poking around. Scientific instruments onboard reveal that Mars was once a warm and wet planet. Did ancient Martians have Slip 'N Slides?

Did You Know?

During the war, General George Washington and his men used invisible ink to send one another secret messages written in letters or on the backs of books.

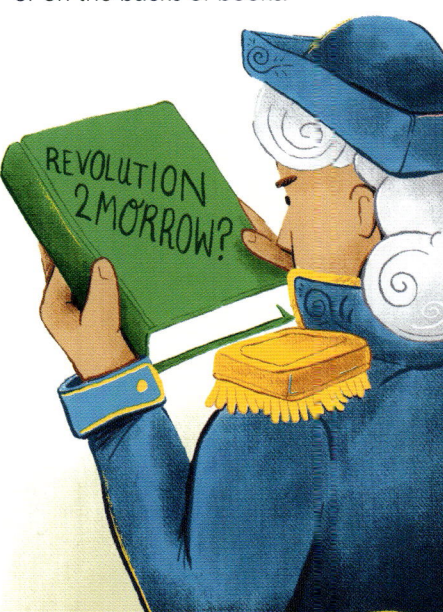

REVOLUTION 2MORROW?

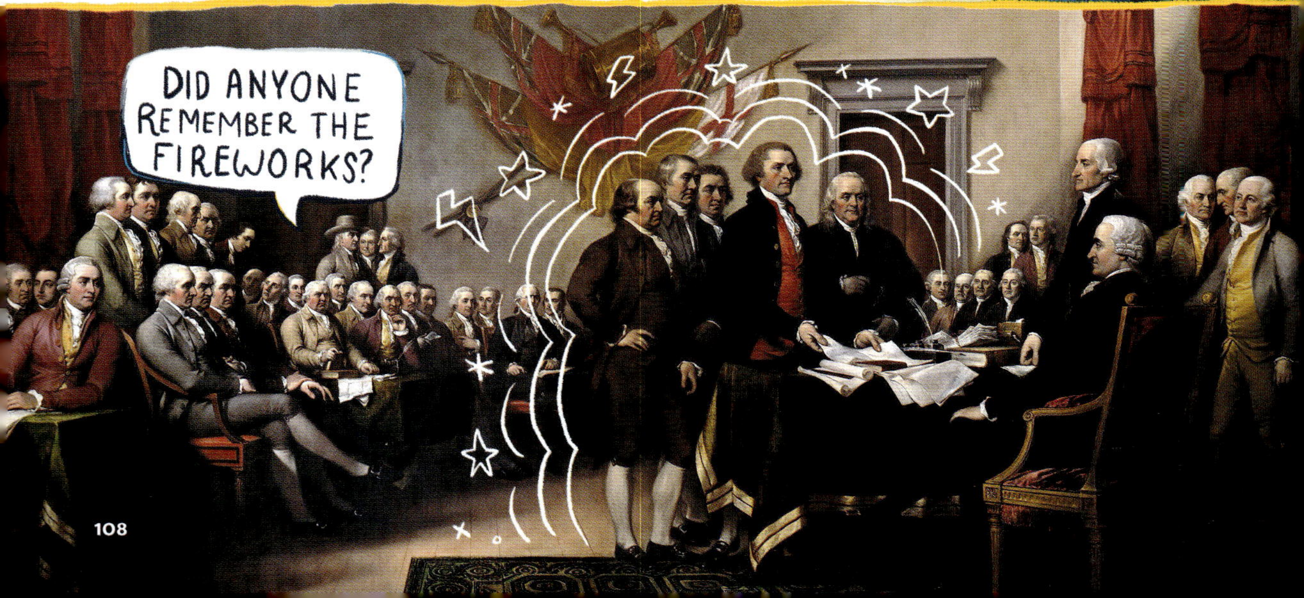
DID ANYONE REMEMBER THE FIREWORKS?

1865 • The U.S. Secret Service begins operation, originally focused on stopping criminals from counterfeiting money. How do they do that? It's a secret—*duh.*

1879 • An almost-complete skeleton of an extinct mastodon is uncovered near Newburgh, New York, after a farmer gives his son a chore to dig a ditch. Can you imagine what you might find if you ever cleaned your room?

1994 • Jeff Bezos founds amazon.com. The company goes on to make him one of the richest people in the world. Depending on things like the stock market and company performance, the list of who is the number one richest person often changes. So Jeff, don't worry! If you aren't number one at this moment, there's always tomorrow!

1996 • **Dolly the sheep is born—the first successfully cloned mammal.** Having an exact copy of yourself must be weird, but it is also a great way to save money on mirrors.

JULY 6

1785 • **That name is *money*! Congress unanimously resolves to name the U.S. currency the dollar.**

1885 • Two days after being bitten by a rabid dog, 9-year-old Joseph Meister is treated with the world's first anti-rabies vaccine, created by scientist Louis Pasteur and his team of experts. This begins the modern age of lifesaving immunization treatments.

2020 • Kansas City Chiefs quarterback Patrick Mahomes signs the largest contract in pro football history: a 12-year deal worth over half a billion dollars. If you're friends with Pat this would be a good time to ask him to buy you a new football.

2016 • Pokemon Go launches in the App Store and Google Play. At its peak, the game had 232 million active players around the world. It's fun, but as government agencies had to warn users, it's also potentially dangerous. There was a report of two players who were so fixated on the virtual world on their phone screens that they walked off a cliff!

NAME IDEAS for $$$
1. AMERICASH
2. REPUBLIBUCKS
3. DOLLARS?

JULY 7

1947 • **The Air Force releases a statement to the press that has everyone looking up for visitors from outer space.** They announced that they had recovered a large "flying disc" that appeared to have crashed on a ranch near Roswell, New Mexico. That's right—the U.S. government said it had found a flying saucer! Over the years, there has been speculation that the recovered craft might have been a high-tech weather balloon or a spy plane from the Soviet Union. But those things aren't nearly as fun as believing it was the wreck of aliens who obviously needed driving lessons.

What Is Area 51?

Area 51 is a supersecret U.S. Air Force installation in Nevada that does not allow visitors from the general public (or outer space) to enter. Many conspiracy theorists believe that the base is used to house and test the alien technology that was recovered at Roswell.

1954 • Ford Motor Company puts together a team and sets them to work on designing a new car brand—the Edsel. When it was released, the vehicles' sales drove straight into the toilet. Edsel was a massive failure, with consumers calling the cars ugly and overpriced and car experts saying they were poorly made. It was such a flop that Edsel became shorthand for describing a product that stinks.

2017 • The 7/7 attacks, four coordinated terrorist bombings, take place in London's transit system. That terrible morning, 52 innocent people were killed and nearly 800 injured.

JULY 8

1497 • Portuguese navigator Vasco da Gama leaves on his first voyage, eventually becoming the first European to reach India by sailing around Africa. Before that, traders traveled by the Silk Road, a trade route from eastern China to the Mediterranean Sea, which was riddled with natural and criminal hazards.

1776 • *Bong!* **The 2,000-pound bell now known as the Liberty Bell rings out for the first time in Philadelphia.** It got its big famous crack when it was rung to celebrate Washington's birthday in 1846 and was retired.

2011 • Snapchat launches from founder Evan Spiegel's father's living room. It was originally called Picaboo. Cute!

1762 • Catherine the Great becomes the ruler of Russia after leading a coup against the czar, who happened to be her husband, Peter III. Two things most people don't know about Russia's Catherine the Great: 1. Her birth name wasn't Catherine (it was Sophie). 2. She wasn't Russian. She was born in the German kingdom of Prussia.

1981 • **Nintendo releases its hit video game Donkey Kong**, which features an ape throwing barrels and a funny little Italian guy gamers will one day come to know as Mario. Yes, *that* Mario.

2001 • TV premiere of *The Office*, which was originally a show in the U.K. starring Ricky Gervais and Martin Freeman (Bilbo Baggins in the *Hobbit* movies). The U.S. remake of the show, starring Steve Carrel in Ricky's role, debuts in 2005, and based on its success, 12 other countries all make their own version. Can the world handle that many Michael Scotts?

JULY 10

925 • The famous Scopes Monkey Trial begins. The trial involved high school science teacher John Thomas Scopes being accused of violating Tennessee state law for teaching the theory of evolution. It was the first court case to be broadcast live on the radio nationwide. Scopes was found guilty and ordered to pay a $100 fine—about $1,700 today. The verdict was overturned on a technicality.

1999 • **After the game goes into penalty kicks, Brandi Chastain fires in a goal that cements Team U.S.A.'s victory over China in the FIFA Women's World Cup.** The win (and Brandi's celebration by tearing off her jersey) became an iconic moment for women's sports.

2018 • Some 200-million-year-old fossils of the earliest known giant dinosaur, the *Ingentia prima*, are found in Argentina. Paleontologists believe it was 33 feet long and weighed about 10 tons. But as scary as that sounds, the only thing that lived in fear of this beast was a bunch of ferns. The *Ingentia prima* was a plant eater.

JULY 11

The date is 7/11, get it?

BRAIN-FREEZE

1804 • In one of the most famous duels in world history, Vice President Aaron Burr shoots and mortally wounds Alexander Hamilton, one of Washington's right-hand men during the Revolutionary War and America's first Secretary of Treasury. The duel was the result of decades of personal and political arguments between the two coming to a boiling point. Despite having committed murder, Burr returned to Washington, D.C., where he remained until the charges were dropped.

1960 • One of the most gripping and beloved books ever written, *To Kill a Mockingbird* by Harper Lee, is published.

2022 • NASA's James Webb Space Telescope gives us the deepest view of the universe ever seen, revealing thousands of galaxies in just one tiny patch of sky.

JULY 12

1923 • The iconic Hollywood Sign is completed in the hills above Hollywood, California. The 50-feet-tall letters originally said "Hollywoodland," but the four last letters were dropped when it was renovated in 1949.

2013 • **It's Malala Day, dedicated to the amazing resilience of Malala Yousafzai!** In 2012, Malala was shot by a Taliban gunman on the bus on her way home from school in Pakistan. The gunman didn't believe women should be allowed to be educated. Nine months after being shot, on her 16th birthday, Malala delivered a powerful speech at the U.N., calling on world leaders to ensure safe and free education for children around the world. At the age of 17, Malala became the youngest person to receive the Nobel Peace Prize.

1871 — The first official cat show is held in London's Crystal Palace. Over 20,000 attendees rushed to see which feline would, *um*, lick the competition and win.

1985 — **The Live Aid concert kicks off** in England and continues in Philadelphia. The 16-hour mega-show featured the most famous musicians on the planet and raised more than $125 million for famine relief in Ethiopia.

2013 — Alicia Garza posts a message on Facebook with the phrase "Black lives matter" after George Zimmerman is acquitted of killing a Black teenager named Trayvon Martin in 2012. The phrase becomes a rallying cry for a social justice movement around the world.

2015 — The musical *Hamilton*, written by and starring Lin-Manuel Miranda, opens in previews on Broadway and goes on to break nearly every Broadway box office record. Who knew that the founding fathers were such good rappers?

JULY 14

789 — **IT'S BASTILLE DAY!** The French Revolution begins with the storming of the Bastille prison by citizens who want to overthrow the corrupt and uncaring monarchy. Political prisoners were freed; weapons and ammunition looted. The day is celebrated every year as a time when common citizens rose up against cruel tyranny.

1943 — **A National Monument in Missouri is dedicated to George Washington Carver**, an amazing man who survived slavery as a child and went on to become one of the most respected agricultural scientists in the world. Carver created more than 300 food and commercial products that came from peanuts, including milk, steak sauce, drinks, cooking oils, salad oil, paper, cosmetics, soaps, and wood stains.

⭐ It's National Mac & Cheese Day!

The first known recipe for this ooey-gooey delight appeared in an Italian cookbook written in the 14th century. Thomas Jefferson is credited for popularizing it in the United States, which is a close second to his other accomplishment—writing the Declaration of Independence.

JULY 15

1858 • Hold your nose while reading! The British Parliament passes a bill to keep people from dumping waste in the Thames River to stop what came to be known in London as the Great Stink. A superhot summer turned the waterway into what writer Amy Chandler described as "a bubbling vat of stench and raw sewage that contributed to outbreaks of disease." We hope the bill also discouraged people from swimming in it!

1890 • English game inventor David Foster files his patent for table tennis. The original setup involved stringed rackets and kept evolving until it became the game we know today as Ping-Pong. By the way, the name *ping-pong* comes from the sound the ball makes when it is batted back and forth.

★ It's National Gummi Worm Day!

A German candy company called Trolli introduced this treat to America in 1981 with the goal of getting kids' attention and grossing out their parents. Success on both fronts!

JULY 16

1945 • **At 5:29 in the morning, the first atom bomb is successfully tested in the desert of New Mexico.** The explosion created a huge mushroom cloud that went 40,000 feet into the air. Watching the cloud rise, J. Robert Oppenheimer, the lead scientist who directed the invention of the bomb, was overheard uttering a phrase from Hindu scripture: "Now I am become Death, the destroyer of worlds."

2002 • President George W. Bush announces the creation of the Department of Homeland Security to protect America from terrorist attacks.

2017 • Roger Federer wins his eighth Wimbledon singles title, setting a record. The only thing this guy loved more than playing tennis was winning at tennis.

1955 • Disneyland opens on 160 acres of what used to be orange groves in Anaheim, California. It cost $17 million to build back then. Today, Disneyland is visited by about 18 million Mickey Mouse superfans every year, who spend around $3 billion to go on super-fun rides and wait on not-so-super-fun lines.

❓ Did You Know?

According to lore, a welder named George died during the construction of the Pirates of the Caribbean ride at the Magic Kingdom Park in Florida. Legend is that his ghost haunts the ride, and every night at closing time, ride workers say, "Goodnight, George."

JULY 18

64 • An intense fire begins in the slums of ancient Rome and quickly spreads because of the high winds. By the time it burned out, nearly 70 percent of the city lay in ruins. There is a famous expression about how Rome's Emperor Nero handled the situation: Nero played the fiddle while Rome burned. But historians say this can't be true for two reasons: Nero wasn't in Rome when the fire broke out and the fiddle wasn't yet invented.

1863 • Formerly enslaved Union Army soldier William Harvey Carney takes part in the Civil War Battle of Fort Wagner. After his regiment's color guard (the person carrying the American flag) was shot, Carney grabbed the flag and carried it up the hill, urging his fellow troops to follow in the attack. Carney was shot multiple times during the battle and survived. His act of bravery and leadership was the earliest by a Black soldier to be later recognized with the Medal of Honor, which Carney received in 1900.

1976 • **The 14-year-old gymnast Nadia Comaneci scores the first perfect 10 in Olympic gymnastics.** The scoreboard actually read "1.0" because the scoreboard builders never expected it to have to display a perfect score and so it didn't have enough digits to display "10.0."

JULY 19

★ **It's National Hot Dog Day!**

Here are five juicy tidbits about the sizzling snack.

1. Many historians believe the birthplace of hot dogs (or frankfurters) was Frankfurt, Germany.

2. *Apollo 7* astronauts ate hot dogs on their way to the moon.

3. Between backyard barbecues and ball games, approximately 20 billion hot dogs are consumed in America every year.

4. Competitive eater Joey Chestnut holds the world hot dog–eating record— gobbling 76 Nathan's Famous hot dogs and buns in 10 minutes.

5. The most expensive hot dog in the world was served at the restaurant 230 Fifth in New York City. Made of the world's most expensive steak, dry-aged Japanese wagyu beef, this dog cost $2,300!

1799 • **During Napoleon Bonaparte's Egyptian campaign, a French soldier discovers a strange black basalt slab inscribed with ancient writing near the town of Rosetta.** It had fragments of passages written in three different languages: Greek, Egyptian hieroglyphics, and Egyptian demotic. The Greek passage explained that all three passages were the same, and so archaeologists were able to use this artifact, the Rosetta stone, to finally unlock the mystery of hieroglyphics, a written language that had been dead for nearly 1,500 years.

1903 • **The first Tour de France bicycle race ends** with French rider Maurice Garin taking home the trophy. Of the 60 riders who began the brutal 1,500-mile race, only 21 finished. There were flat tires, injuries, and one guy even fell asleep mid-race!

1945 • Nearly 1,000 athletes with special needs compete in the first Special Olympics. Today, the organization helps millions of people with intellectual disabilities get healthier, overcome isolation and injustice—and have fun!

1969 • **Astronaut Neil Armstrong is the first human to step foot onto the surface of the moon.** He and fellow astronaut Buzz Aldrin spend 21 and a half hours up there (which includes seven hours of trying to nap) before rejoining third mission member Michael Collins in the Command Module and heading home. Because there is no wind on the moon, that first footprint is still there!

2018 • U.S. daredevil athlete Aaron Fotheringham sets three wheelchair stunt records in one day—including the longest wheelchair ramp jump, which sent him soaring 70 feet!

2021 • Amazon billionaire Jeff Bezos and three others blast off on a suborbital flight on Blue Origin's *New Shepard* rocket, setting a bunch of records in the process: the oldest person to fly to space, the first siblings in space at the same time, the youngest person to go to space, and the first suborbital spacecraft to carry paying customers.

JULY **21**

🚩 It's National Junk Food Day!

The term *junk food* was popularized by Michael Jacobson, director of the Center for Science in the Public Interest, who used it for the first time in 1972. Junk foods (such as candy and sodas) are very high in calories and sugar. Delicious but not nutritious!

❓ Did You Know?

The inventor of the first cotton-candy machine was also a dentist. Guess he wanted to make sure his cavity drilling business had a steady stream of customers.

FREE *with* EVERY CLEANING!

1865 • The first Wild West one-on-one quick-draw showdown occurs between Wild Bill Hickok and Davis Tutt. Wild Bill walks away triumphant. And Tutt? Well, he didn't walk anywhere after that.

1904 • After more than a decade of construction, the world's longest railroad is nearly complete. Today, the Trans-Siberian Railway runs 5,772 miles from Europe to the far end of Asia. Not recommended if you're in a rush—end to end, the trip takes about seven days.

2012 • Motors, *schmotors*! Adventurer Erden Eruç completes the first solo trip around the world using only muscle power. The dude rowed, kayaked, hiked, and cycled this incredible—and incredibly tiring—journey that lasted, by his time keeping, five years, 11 days, 12 hours, and 22 minutes. (Can you tell he really, really wanted it to be over?)

What Is a Solar Eclipse?

A solar eclipse happens when the orbit of the moon puts it directly between the earth and the sun, throwing a shadow on the earth and blackening the sky for observers. In 709 BCE, a Chinese astronomer wrote one of the first-known descriptions of a solar eclipse: "The sun was eclipsed; it was total." Brief but accurate! Serious note: Never ever look directly at an eclipse because it can damage your eyes.

1933 After nearly eight days soaring in the sky, American aviator Wiley Post touches his airplane down in New York's Floyd Bennett Field and becomes the first pilot to fly solo around the globe.

2009 Who turned out the lights? On this day, **the longest total solar eclipse of the 21st century is observed**, lasting six minutes and 39 seconds.

JULY **23**

2015 **NASA announces that they've found earth's cousin! Located 1,400 light-years away, the planet is called Kepler-452b** (sheesh, NASA, couldn't you think of a catchier namet?). It is about earth's size and orbits in what they described as a "habitable zone" around a star much like our sun. That means it is where liquid water can exist on the surface of the planet, supporting life (and extraterrestrial water-balloon fights).

How Far Is a Light-Year?

Short answer: very far! Long answer: 5.88 trillion miles. In the vacuum of space, light travels 186,000 miles per second, and a light-year is how far it would get in a year.

2021 The 2020 Summer Olympic Games start...in 2021. After being postponed because of the COVID-19 pandemic, the Olympic torch was finally relit. Surfing and skateboarding made their debut at the games. Japanese skateboarding star Yuto Horigome won the men's street skateboarding gold, which is ironic because the town he grew up in still has "No Skateboarding" signs posted on a lot of its streets.

1567 ● Mary Queen of Scots is forced to abdicate (give up her throne), and her 1-year-old son becomes King James VI of Scotland. We hope he was potty-trained before they let him sit on the throne.

1847 ● On what is known as Pioneer Day to the Church of Jesus Christ of Latter-Day Saints, Brigham Young founds Salt Lake City after leading a treacherous thousand-mile exodus of followers from Illinois that involved crossing the Rocky Mountains in horse- and ox-drawn wagons (no SUVs back then). Some smaller wagons were pulled by people!

1911 ● **While climbing atop a mountain ridge in Peru, Yale University history professor Hiram Bingham III stumbles upon ruins on an ancient Incan estate called Machu Picchu.** The site stretches over five miles with more than 3,000 stone steps that link together its many sections. No one knows exactly why it was abandoned—it was never attacked by conquistadors—but historians theorize that a smallpox epidemic must have wiped out its residents around 1530.

Who Were the Incas?

The Incas ruled a vast empire in the Andes mountain region of South America. They were known for their sophisticated agricultural and roadway system, as well as a religious belief system that sometimes involved animal or human sacrifice. In 1572, the empire was overtaken by Spanish invaders who brought superior weapons and terrible diseases with them from Europe.

1944 ● **The Aztec Eagles Squadron is activated.** This was Mexico's elite Air Force squadron, which was trained by the United States and flew dangerous missions against the Japanese during the liberation of the Philippines.

What Was the War of 1812?

The three-year-long war was fought between the United States and Great Britain. The British were blockading American ships to stop them from trading with France. They captured the American crew members and forced them to join the British side. Native Americans, whose lands were being invaded by U.S. troops, sided with the British in the war. While a coalition of Native Americans under the leadership of Tecumseh fought many successful battles, America's eventual victory against the British destroyed the Native Americans' chances of putting up a unified front against the U.S.'s expansion into their territories.

1814 The War of 1812's Battle of Niagara Falls takes place: Canadian and British troops repel invading U.S. forces. (That's right, America tried to invade Canada!)

1978 The birth of the world's first test-tube baby occurs in England. The baby, Louise Brown, wasn't actually born inside a tube: The now common process, called in vitro fertilization (IVF), involves an embryo being transferred to a mother's womb after being fertilized in a laboratory.

1999 Cyclist Lance Armstrong wins his first of seven consecutive wins at the Tour de France. He later has his titles stripped away after being accused of cheating with the use of performance-enhancing drugs.

1775 The U.S. postal system officially starts with Benjamin Franklin as its first postmaster general. In 1847, Congress authorized the first two United States postage stamps. One had George Washington's profile, and the other, you guessed it, featured Ben.

1931 An apocalyptic swarm of grasshoppers descends on America's Midwest, devouring millions of acres of crops.

1943 Dense fumes blanket Los Angeles in what is feared to be a chemical attack from Japan. Turns out the culprit isn't an enemy attack; it's pollution. The combination of fog, factory smoke, and car exhaust had enveloped L.A. in a thick smog.

JULY 26

❓ Did You Know?

The rarest stamp in the world is the British Guiana One-Cent Magenta. It was made in 1856 and has been described as "the *Mona Lisa* of the stamp world." A stamp dealer named Stanley Gibbons bought it in an auction in 2021 for $8.3 million!

1377 • Following a plague outbreak, the port of Dubrovnik in Croatia institutes the first known state-imposed quarantine.

1940 • "What's up, doc?" Bugs Bunny makes his rascally debut in a short called "A Wild Hare."

What Is Plague?

Plague is a deadly illness that usually spreads through bites from fleas that previously bit an infected animal. There are actually three variations: bubonic, pneumonic, and septicemic. In the 1300s, a devastating outbreak of bubonic plague, also called Black Death, killed millions of people in Europe, Asia, and North Africa. Plague still exists, but it is extremely rare.

Better Know Your Bugs

1. The name Bugs Bunny came from artist and animator Ben "Bugs" Hardaway. When he was doodling a new rabbit character, one of his coworkers referred to the drawing as "Bugs's Bunny."

2. His signature phrase "What's up, Doc?" was a common expression in Texas, so animator and director Tex Avery didn't think much of having Bugs say it. Little did he know it would become an iconic phrase remembered for decades to come.

3. The voice of Bugs Bunny came from actor Mel Blanc, who also voiced tons of other Looney Tunes characters, including Daffy Duck, Tweety Bird, Speedy Gonzales, and Marvin the Martian. Plus, he was Barney Rubble in *The Flintstones*.

2021 • **Simone Biles, one of the greatest gymnasts of all time, announces she is stepping away from competition in the middle of the Olympics,** citing the importance of self-care. She told reporters, "I have to do what is right for me and focus on my mental health and not jeopardize my health and my well-being."

JULY 28

1868 • The 14th Amendment is added to the U.S. Constitution, granting citizenship to all people born or naturalized in the United States—including formerly enslaved people—and guarantees these citizens "equal protection of the laws."

1914 • One month after the assassination of Archduke Franz Ferdinand, Austria-Hungary declares war on Serbia, which begins World War I.

2021 • **Astrophysicists observe light coming from behind a black hole.** So what? This offers yet another proof of Einstein's theory of general relativity, which states that gravity warps space. Man, that guy was smart!

JULY 29

1954 • **Fantasy writer J.R.R. Tolkien publishes the first part of his epic *The Lord of the Rings* trilogy.** The books were inspired in part by myths fables, and religious texts, as well as by Tolkien's experiences fighting in the British army during World War I.

1958 • The National Aeronautics and Space Administration (NASA) is created to launch (pun intended) America's space program.

? Did You Know?

Tolkien was obsessed with language. In his novels, he didn't just write gibberish when the elves and other creatures speak; he invented actual languages for them with grammatical rules. Just think, you could actually study and become fluent in Orcish.

1945 — Shortly after delivering parts of the atomic bomb that would later be dropped on Hiroshima, the United States Navy heavy cruiser USS *Indianapolis* is hit by a Japanese submarine attack. Nine hundred men were able to abandon ship into the Pacific Ocean before it sank. But by the time they were rescued four days later, only 316 had survived—the water was shark-infested and they suffered near-constant attacks.

1948 — Coming in off the top rope, it's pro wrestling, which makes its punchy, piledriving premiere on prime-time TV.

2011 — **The first International Day of Friendship is declared by the United Nations.** Did you know that friendship isn't just fun? It has been scientifically proven to be good for you, mentally and physically. That's right, doctors say you and your friends should goof off together for your health!

2016 — Look out below! On this day, Luke Aikins jumps out of a plane at an altitude of 25,000 feet without a parachute—on purpose—and lands safely in a giant net below. Thank goodness he had good aim.

YOU HAVE **1** NEW FRIEND REQUEST!

EARTH, THE
7.9 BILLION FRIENDS IN COMMON

APPROVE   DENY

JULY 31

VRROOM! VRROOM!

1752 — The Vienna Zoo opens in Austria—and has yet to close its doors. It is the oldest zoo in operation.

1971 — ***Apollo 15* astronauts David Scott and James Irwin go for a cruise on the surface of the moon, driving the Lunar Roving Vehicle.** It's the first off-planet joyride ever.

1975 — In one of the most famous unsolved missing-persons cases in history, labor leader Jimmy Hoffa goes out to eat at a restaurant with some associates and disappears. His car is found in the restaurant parking lot, but he is never heard from or seen again. Most believe he was the victim of a Mafia hit, but there was never any evidence to prove what happened.

THIS DAY IN *my* HISTORY
JULY

Fill in any memorable events from your life here.

1

2

3

4

5

6

7

8

9

10

11

12

13

14

15

16

17

18

19

20

21

22

23

24

25

26

27

28

29

30

31

AUGUST 1

1981
MTV debuts at 12:01 a.m., with one of the channel's creators, John Lack, declaring, "Ladies and gentlemen, rock and roll." While MTV was a powerhouse that defined popular music for decades, it also created reality TV as we know it with shows like *The Real World* and *Jersey Shore*. Whether that is a good or a terrible thing is up to you to decide.

1984
A worker in England who is harvesting peat in a bog called Lindow Moss spots what he thinks is a piece of wood. It turns out to be a human leg! More digging around uncovered the remains of a man who would be known as Lindow Man. Scientific analysis determined that he lived as early as 1 CE and that he was murdered, making it a more than 2,000-year-old cold case.

AUGUST 2

A food vendor named Jerry Newberg claimed he invented the ice cream sandwich in 1945 and sold them at Pittsburgh's Forbes Field during baseball games. His claim might not be totally true, as there are many instances of ice cream sandwiches being mentioned in writing before that date. However, what is 100 percent true is that they are delicious.

1990
Iraqi forces invade Kuwait, a small oil-rich nation, sparking the first Gulf War.

2018
TikTok becomes available worldwide. It has become the most downloaded app in history, with more than 3.5 billion users. It's fun, but a little freaky. The FBI warned that the app could be used to spy on users through their devices. Yikes!

AUGUST 3

1492 • Explorer Christopher Columbus sets sail from Spain commanding three ships, the *Niña*, *Pinta*, and *Santa María*. He was searching for an all-water route to India but made landfall on a Caribbean Island. Believing he had reached the Far East, Columbus called the indigenous people he encountered Indians. It is an inaccurate name that stuck for centuries.

1958 • **The American nuclear submarine USS *Nautilus* becomes the first vessel to reach the North Pole** after traveling 1,000 miles beneath Arctic ice. "That is one weird-looking whale," thought a nearby polar bear.

1984 • The 4'9" U.S. gymnast Mary Lou Retton needs a perfect 10 score to win the all-around gymnastic at the Olympics. She nails it on her first attempt, and then just for fun vaults again, earning a second perfect 10. You don't have to be tall to create big moments in history!

AUGUST 4

1945 • As a gesture of friendship between the allies of World War II, the Soviet Union gives a hand-carved statue of the Great Seal of the United States to U.S. ambassador Averell Harriman. Nice, right? Wrong. The gift, which Harriman hung in his study, had a spy bug in it, and the Soviet Union used it to listen in on secret conversations for seven years before it was discovered. Known as The Thing by the CIA experts who examined it, the spy bug was the first known one—but it certainly wasn't the last.

2006 • Travis Pastrana performs a double backflip at the X Games. If that doesn't sound too impressive, we should add that he was riding a motorcycle at the time.

2020 • President Donald Trump signs the Great American Outdoors Act, which provides massive funding for national parks, wildlife refuges, and Native American schools.

It's National Chocolate Chip Cookie Day!

There was once a terrible time in history when chocolate chip cookies didn't exist—and then a chef named Ruth Wakefield had a big idea. She chipped a bunch of chocolate and added it to a dough mix, expecting it to melt and create an all-chocolate cookie. But the chocolate chips remained intact as they baked, resulting in an all-new cookie. She named it the Toll House chocolate crunch cookie after the Toll House Inn restaurant that she ran in Massachusetts. Best invention ever?

AUGUST 5

1914 · **Before this day, it was impossible to run a red light—because there weren't any.** But on this day, based on a design by James Hoge, the first electric traffic light in the United States is installed on the corner of East 105th Street and Euclid Avenue in Cleveland.

1993 · Finally, a way for good friends to attack one another with swords and spells and no one gets hurt! Magic: The Gathering trading-card game is launched, blazing the way for games like Pokémon and Yu-Gi-Oh!

2013 · Mars rover *Curiosity* plays "Happy Birthday" to celebrate its first year on the red planet. It was the first time that music had been played on a planet other than earth, but sadly, no Martian bakeries were open, so *Curiosity* didn't get any birthday cake.

AUGUST 6

1945 · In the first and only use of atomic weapons in warfare, the U.S. B-29 Superfortress *Enola Gay* drops the atomic bomb, code-named Little Boy, on Hiroshima in Japan. Three days later, the U.S. drops a second atomic bomb, called Fat Man. The bombs leave total devastation behind them, killing more than 100,000 people instantly and tens of thousands later from radiation poisoning. Six days after the bombing, the emperor of Japan officially surrendered on what would be known as V-J Day.

1991 · The world's first website goes live. Info.cern.ch was created by British computer scientist Tim Berners-Lee to share information about the World Wide Web. It's still live today!

AUGUST 7

1782 · General George Washington creates the Badge of Military Merit. It becomes known as the Purple Heart, which continues to be awarded to any soldier who has been wounded or killed in action while serving.

1974 · **French tightrope walker Phillippe Petit** walks across a wire strung between the 1,350-foot-high towers of the World Trade Center with no net—and no permission. He was arrested on the other side.

2021 · With 11 medals around her neck, American runner Allyson Felix becomes the most decorated U.S. track and field athlete of all time.

AUGUST 8

1974 ● **President Richard M. Nixon announces that he is resigning**, making him the first president in American history to quit. He does this to avoid being impeached for the Watergate scandal, which involved men from his reelection team breaking into the office of the Democratic National Committee to steal documents and tap their phones. No wonder he earned the nickname Tricky Dick.

What Is an Impeachment?

Although it usually gets discussed about presidents, impeachment is part of a process that is used to remove any government official from office (in other words, fire them). If an official is believed to have broken laws or endangered the safety of our nation, the House of Representatives votes to impeach them. If the majority votes yes, they are impeached, and it moves to the Senate, where a two-thirds majority is needed to convict. Only three U.S. presidents—Andrew Johnson, Bill Clinton, and Donald Trump—have been impeached by the House of Representatives, with Trump being the only one to get impeached twice. No one has been convicted by the Senate and kicked out of the White House...yet.

1992 ● The U.S. Men's basketball team, The Dream Team, takes the gold medal at the Olympics. The games were never even close—they beat Angola 116-48—and many of their competitors asked them for autographs after the games.

2009 ● Sonia Sotomayor is sworn in as an associate justice of the Supreme Court. Born in the Bronx to Puerto Rican parents, she is the first Hispanic justice and third woman to serve on the nation's highest court.

AUGUST 9

1845 ● American writer and philosopher Henry David Thoreau's classic book *Walden: or Life in the Woods* is published. The book details Thoreau's decision to live in nature for two years and becomes a guide to finding purpose and happiness by living simply and appreciating our surroundings.

1936 ● **At the Berlin Olympics, Black track star Jesse Owens wins his fourth gold medal** in the 4-by-100-meter relay and his team sets a new world record. Owen's multiple wins were a punch in the face to Nazi leader Adolf Hitler, who planned to use the Berlin Games to demonstrate the so-called superiority of the Aryan race.

1937 ● The Electro String Corporation patents the first electric guitar, called the Rickenbacker Frying Pan. It sounds different from acoustic guitars, and it is way, way louder!

1962 ● It's the birthday of Suzanne Collins, author of *The Hunger Games* series. If she invites you to a backyard party and starts handing out weapons, we recommend you run!

1962 ● **Amazing Fantasy #15 marks the first appearance of everyone's favorite web-head, Spider-Man.** (Well, everyone except the Green Goblin.)

★ It's National S'Mores Day!

The first known recipe for this ooey-gooey treat was published in a 1927 Girl Scout guidebook. The name is short for *some more*, as in "gimme some more!"

AUGUST 11

1934 ● **A group of federal prisoners designated as "most dangerous" arrives at Alcatraz, a prison built on a 22-acre rocky island in San Francisco Bay.** The guards, barbed wire, and frigid water surrounding it make it one of the most secure prisons on earth. Infamous criminals like Al Capone and George "Machine Gun" Kelly were locked up within its walls.

2019 ● The 21-year-old race car driver Jamie Chadwick wins the first W Series, a new women-only Formula 3 racing league.

Escape from Alcatraz

Many prisoners tried and failed to escape Alcatraz. But in 1962, a trio of convicts did get out thanks to a wild plan. They used sharpened spoons they stole from the prison cafeteria to dig through the air vents in their cells. Then, to fool the passing guards, they left dummy heads in their beds that they made from paper, soap, and human hair from the prison barbershop. Finally, they built a raft and life preservers, using instructions they had read in *Popular Mechanics* magazine and about 50 raincoats they stole or received as gifts from their fellow inmates. Today, the FBI keeps active arrest warrants for the three men, but they are presumed to have died in the strong currents of the bay.

AUGUST 12

Three Ferocious Facts About *T. Rex*

1. The name *Tyrannosaurus rex* is a combination of Greek and Latin words meaning "tyrant lizard king."

2. They had 50 to 60 banana-size teeth that could tear away hundreds of pounds of meat in a single bite.

3. Its tiny arms might look puny, but they were likely handy in attacks, able to deliver devastating slashes in up-close-and-personal fights.

1981 — IBM introduces its first personal computer (PC) that is created to be used in the home. A full home operating system cost about $3,000 back then, which is about $10,000 in today's money.

1990 — While exploring a cliff outside of Faith, South Dakota, fossil hunter Susan Hendrickson notices three huge bones sticking out of the rock. After excavation the bones turn out to be part of **the largest *Tyrannosaurus rex* skeleton ever discovered.** The 65-million-year-old specimen was named Sue after its finder. Not just huge, the skeleton was amazingly intact and taught paleontologists tons about the nine-ton beast. Sue's skeleton includes a wishbone, supporting the growing scientific consensus that birds are actually a type of living dinosaur.

AUGUST 13

1918 — At the age of 40, Opha May Johnson is the first woman to enlist in the Marine Corps. She worked her way up to the rank of sergeant during World War I.

1860 — **It's the birthday of Wild West icon and sharpshooter Annie Oakley.** Her ability to perform incredible trick shots brought her worldwide fame in Buffalo Bill's Wild West Show. She performed for kings and queens, and in 1894, Oakley starred in Thomas Edison's kinetoscope film *The Little Sure Shot of the Wild West*, which featured her speedily shooting little glass balls that were tossed into the air one by one.

1961 — Construction of the Berlin Wall begins. East German soldiers created a barbed wire and brick barrier between Soviet-controlled East Berlin and democratic West Berlin. The stated purpose was that the wall would keep West Berliners from invading, but the truth is that the wall was built to keep East Berliners from escaping.

AUGUST 14

1935 President Franklin D. Roosevelt signs the Social Security Act, which establishes a system for financially supporting American citizens in their old age.

2003 Who turned off the lights? **The worst blackout in North American history hits the northeastern U.S.** and southern Canada, leaving 50 million people without any electricity for up to 24 hours. "That must have been tough," said a caveman who didn't have any power his entire lifetime.

AUGUST 15

DO YOU LIKE THIS BAND?

IT'S JUST NOT MY KIND of MOOSIC.

1914 The Panama Canal, a 50-mile man-made waterway that connects the Atlantic and Pacific oceans, officially opens. More than one million ships have used the canal since it opened, saving time and the danger of sailing all the way down and around South America, which has some of the most treacherous and choppiest waters on earth around its southern tip.

1969 Lots of cows hear rock and roll music for the first time as the **Woodstock music festival opens** on a patch of farmland in upstate New York. The legendary cultural event featured some of the biggest musical artists of the time. The only thing it lacked was good planning: The concert organizers thought about 50,000 people would show up—but about 500,000 did. There wasn't enough food or shelter or portable toilets, and everyone was soaked with rain, but the three-day festival defined the Peace and Love Generation. No incidents of violence occurred, and two babies were born!

AUGUST 16

We know not all jokes are hilarious, but did you hear the one about the Liberty Bell? It really cracked us up! (We'll wait for you to stop groaning.)

1896 George Carmack goes salmon fishing in a creek near the Klondike River in Canada's Yukon Territory and catches a whole lot more than dinner. He notices nuggets of gold beneath the water, and once word gets out, the last great gold rush begins. Thousands of gold seekers head north with Klondike Fever, encouraged by the news of the arrival in San Francisco of two steamships from the Yukon carrying two tons of gold.

1994 Before there was the iPhone there was the IBM Simon. The world's first smartphone had a lot of cool functions, but two big downsides stopped it from taking off: It was big and clunky, weighing over a pound. And its battery lasted only about an hour.

2008 Jamaican sprinter Usain Bolt has the perfect name. Seemingly as fast as lightning, he set a new 100-meter sprint world record of 9.69 seconds at the 2008 Summer Olympics. Then, exactly one year later, he shattered that record by running it in 9.58 seconds. Bolt was zooming at an incredible 23.35 mph, so if he ran by your school during drop-off, he would have gotten a speeding ticket!

AUGUST 17

1908 **The very first animated cartoon, *Fantasmagorie*, is shown in Paris.** The two-minute flick starts with the actual hands of the artist, Emile Cohl, drawing a little guy named Pierrot who springs to life and rides an elephant that turns into a house that becomes a balloon…. Long story short: It is weird!

1959 Nils "Buckle Up" Bohlin files a patent for the three-point seat belt on behalf of Volvo, the company he works for. (By the way, Buckle Up was not actually his nickname.) His seat belts are the same kind we use today, featuring a strap that goes across a passenger's chest. And here's the very cool part: Even though Volvo held the patent, they gave the design away for free to other carmakers to help keep all motorists safe.

AUGUST 18

1590 Creepiest homecoming ever: John White, the governor of the Roanoke Island colony (near what is now North Carolina), returns from England with new supplies and finds the place totally deserted. To this day, no one knows what became of the 100 vanished colonists.

1920 **Tug-of-war is played one final time as an Olympic sport.** (Yes, tug-of-war was once an Olympic sport!) Wonder if anyone tried the ol' "everyone drop the rope at the same time" trick?

1920 After receiving a persuasive note from his mother, **Tennessee State Representative Harry T. Burn casts the deciding vote that ratifies the 19th Amendment to the Constitution**, ensuring women's right to vote.

1934 Roberto Clemente is born in Puerto Rico. He went on to become a professional baseball player and the first Latin American athlete to win the World Series as a starting player. Clemente won a trophy case full of awards and had exactly 3,000 hits during his MLB career. He is also remembered for his charity and advocacy for equality. At age 38, he died tragically in a plane crash while flying from Puerto Rico to Nicaragua to help with earthquake relief.

Dear Son, LET ME VOTE. Love MOM

AUGUST 19

1934 Who needs an engine when you have gravity? **In 1933, car-loving photographer Myron Scott organized a soap box derby for kids in Dayton.** More than 360 kids showed up to race on a downhill course in homemade cars built with soap boxes, scrap wood, baby stroller wheels, and anything else they could get their hands on. It was such a success that Scott was able to get Chevrolet to sponsor the next race, which on this day became the first official All-American Soap Box Derby.

1960 American pilot Gary Powers is sentenced to 10 years in a Soviet prison for espionage. His U-2 spy plane had been shot down on May 1 while flying over Soviet territory. The incident, known as the U-2 Affair, greatly raised the tension between the United States and the Soviet Union. Powers was released two years later in exchange for captured Soviet spy Rudolf Abel.

AUGUST 25

1835 • The first article in a series of six in the *New York Sun* newspaper announces that life was discovered on the moon. The articles described how the moon's surface featured rushing rivers and jungles and was home to unicorns, two-legged beavers, and bat-like humans. If that sounds unbelievable, it's because it is. These articles were meant to be a satire of serious scientific speculation about extraterrestrial life, but people thought they were true. Eventually the newspaper admitted that "The Great Moon Hoax" story was, well, a hoax.

1958 • Entrepreneur Momofuku Ando's company Nissin begins selling instant ramen noodles as a way for people to have cheap, easy-to-make meals. The public slurped it up. Today, billions of bowls of the stuff are made every year.

2006 • How's the weather up there? **Biologists identify the world's tallest tree, named Hyperion.** Located in California's Redwood National Park, the 379-feet-tall Hyperion is believed to be 800 years old. It is so rare that anyone who gets too close to it must pay a $5,000 fine—or possibly go to jail.

2012 • *Voyager 1* becomes first human-made object to reach interstellar space (meaning it left our solar system). That's a long way from home: 11 billion miles away from home, to be specific.

AUGUST 26

1682 • **English astronomer Edmond Halley first observes Halley's comet.** What a coincidence! (Oh wait, they named it after him.) The comet's orbit takes it into earth's neighborhood about once every 75 years. It was last seen in 1986 and should be back in 2061.

1959 • Faced with fuel shortages in Europe, the head of British Motor Corporation, Sir Leonard Lord, set the company in motion to build a small, lightweight car that could go far without needing tons of fuel. The result is as adorable as it is fuel-efficient: The Mini is born!

2020 • In response to the police shooting of Jacob Blake in Kenosha, Wisconsin, professional athletes across all the major leagues—basketball, football, hockey, and soccer—boycotted games and practices to make a statement about the need for social-justice reform.

AUGUST 27

1859 • The oil fields of...Pennsylvania? On this day, retired railroad worker Edwin Laurentine Drake strikes oil by drilling in Titusville, Pennsylvania. Soon after, a guy named John D. Rockefeller cofounded the refinery Standard Oil Company in nearby Ohio, which eventually made him the richest private citizen who ever lived. In today's dollars, by some estimates, he was worth over $300 billion.

1883 • **Krakatoa, a small volcanic island in Indonesia, erupts with a massive explosion**, killing approximately 40,000 people and creating a 120-foot-tall tsunami wave that wiped away several waterfront villages. (The force of the explosion was several times greater than an atomic bomb.)

AUGUST 28

1830 • To prove the superiority of steam engines, a race is held between a steam-powered locomotive and a horse-drawn railroad car. The horse wins after the locomotive breaks down. Oops.

1963 • **Dr. Martin Luther King Jr. delivers his iconic "I Have a Dream" speech** in front of the Lincoln Memorial in Washington, D.C. Standing before a crowd of more than 200,000 people, King explained that he longed for a world where people are not judged "by the color of their skin but by the content of their character." King's speech became a defining moment in the civil rights movement.

2022 • A Mickey Mantle baseball card from 1952 sells at auction for $12,600,000, making it the most expensive baseball card ever sold. The lesson here? Do not throw out your old baseball cards!

AUGUST 29

MOVIE NIGHT!

1997 — **Entrepreneurs Marc Randolph and Reed Hastings launch Netflix, a DVD service that mails movies to subscribers.** Ten years later, the company introduced online streaming; they phased out DVD service in 2023. Still, some people prefer discs. What, they don't think it's fun to scroll through content for hours, then finally settle for an episode of *The Office* they've already seen 20 times?

2005 — Hurricane Katrina makes landfall near New Orleans as a Category 4 hurricane, with winds whipping at 145 mph. While it wasn't the most powerful storm of the Atlantic Hurricane season, floodwalls and levees surrounding the city failed, causing massive flooding throughout the area. Some people in hard-hit neighborhoods were stuck on the roofs of their houses for days until rescuers could get to them; others were less fortunate and drowned in the floodwaters.

CAEDEN

2020 — Born with cerebral palsy, Caeden Thomson's parents were told he would never walk. **But on this day, at the age of 7, Caeden not only walked, he climbed to the top of Ben Nevis, the tallest mountain in Great Britain.**

AUGUST 30

1904 — Marathon runner Fred Lorz finds an amazing way to win the 26.2-mile race. After crossing the finishing line, he admits that when he got a bad cramp, he hitched a ride in a car for 11 miles of the race.

1967 — **Thurgood Marshall becomes the first Black man to be confirmed as a Supreme Court justice.** He served for 24 years, sharing moving insights such as: "The measure of a country's greatness is its ability to retain compassion in times of crisis."

1888 • The body of Jack the Ripper's first murder victim, Mary Ann Nichols, is found in London's East End. For a year, Jack terrorized the city, killing five people in the night and then disappearing before he could be caught. His identity was never uncovered.

1955 • Here's one way to avoid paying high gas prices: **Car engineer William G. Cobb rolls out his 15-inch-long Sunmobile, the world's first solar-powered automobile.** More than 60 years later, no one has figured out how to mass-produce a vehicle that is fueled by sunny days.

15"

1997 • **While racing to try to get away from the paparazzi (photographers) who were harassing and following Princess Diana, her driver crashes in a tunnel in Paris.** Diana, her boyfriend Dodi Al Fayed, and the driver, Henri Paul, died in the accident. Diana became the Princess of Wales when she married Prince Charles, now King Charles III, and maintained that title even after they were divorced. Known for her charitable work, her legacy lives on through an organization called the Diana Award, which aims to support young people trying to make a positive change and impact on the world.

THIS DAY IN *my* HISTORY
AUGUST

Fill in any memorable events from your life here.

1 ....

2 ....

3 ....

4 ....

5 ....

6 ....

7 ....

8 ....

9 ....

10 ....

11 ....

12 ....

13 ....

14 ....

15 ....

16 ....

17 ....

18 ....

19 ....

20 ....

21 ....

22 ....

23 ....

24 ....

25 ....

26 ....

27 ....

28 ....

29 ....

30 ....

31 ....

SEPTEMBER 1

1902 *A Trip to the Moon*, **the first sci-fi film ever, is released in France.** It features a group of travelers who journey on a rocket that hits the moon's face—which is literally a guy's face—right in the eye. It's not exactly *Star Wars*, but it's a start!

1939 One and a half million Nazi troops storm into Poland in an overwhelming invasion from Germany, beginning World War II.

1972 American chess genius Bobby Fischer beats Russian champion Boris Spassky, making him the first American to win the international championship. The match's start was delayed because Fischer had demanded the winner receive a bigger monetary prize. "Bigger check, mate."

1985 *National Geographic* **explorer-in-residence Robert Ballard and French scientist Jean-Louis Michel find the *Titanic*'s remains on the ocean floor 73 years after it sinks.** Large sections of the ship were still recognizable, and in the darkness, the searchers' unmanned submarine found unbroken dinner plates, many pieces of furniture, and even an unopened case of champagne.

2006 Roblox is officially launched by cofounders David Baszucki and Erik Cassel after testing and fine-tuning a version called DynaBlocks they created in 2004. Nearly 60 million people play and create games on the platform Roblox every single day. (But only after they're finished with their homework, right?)

SEPTEMBER 2

1666 — A fire begins in a bakery and due to extremely dry weather conditions, quickly spreads to become the Great Fire of London. More than half of the city burned to the ground, and by the time it was over, 13,200 houses were destroyed. Despite the devastation, only six people are known to have lost their lives.

1945 — **U.S. General Douglas MacArthur accepts Japan's surrender aboard the *USS Missouri* in Tokyo Bay, ending World War II.** Over the course of the war, approximately 60 to 80 million soldiers and civilians lost their lives.

2013 — Super swimmer Diana Nyad, at the age of 64, climbs out of the water in Key West, Florida, having swum the 110 miles from Cuba. If the distance wasn't hard enough, she did it without using a cage to keep her safe in the shark-infested waters. After 53 hours, she emerged with all her fingers and toes intact.

SEPTEMBER 3

1838 — **Future abolitionist leader Frederick Douglass makes his daring escape from slavery** using a disguise and the knowledge he had acquired while forced to work in Baltimore's shipyards. Douglass became a fierce campaigner to end slavery, and his writing and lectures advocated for equality and human rights for all.

1838 — *Shang-Chi and the Legend of the Ten Rings* premieres publicly, the first flick in the MCU to feature a leading Asian superhero. As Bruce Banner tells Shang-Chi and Katy in the post-credits scene: "Welcome to the circus."

1609 • **Navigator Henry Hudson sails up the river that will one day bear his name, and he and his crew become the first Europeans to map the island of Manhattan.** (Unfortunately, there were no hot-pretzel stands in operation back then.)

1886 • The last major Southwest campaign of the Indian Wars comes to an end as the great Apache leader Geronimo surrenders to U.S. government troops. For 30 years, Geronimo and his warriors fought to protect their homeland in the Southwest but were finally exhausted and outnumbered by the unrelenting troops.

1888 • **George Eastman gets the patent for the first roll-film camera called the Kodak.** Before that, photography involved big pieces of equipment and fragile glass plates. Now anyone who can hold a small boxlike camera and click a button can be a photographer. "Say *cheese!*"

1998 • Stanford University graduates Larry Page and Sergey Brin found a search engine company called Google. If you haven't heard of it, just Google it.

2018 • The FBI recovers a pair of Dorothy's ruby slippers from the 1939 film *The Wizard of Oz* that were stolen from a museum in 2005. They were brought to the Smithsonian in Washington, D.C., for safekeeping. "There's no place like home!"

SEPTEMBER 5

1836 Sam Houston is elected as president of the Republic of Texas after a successful rebellion gave it independence from Mexico. Texas joined the United States in 1845, left the union in 1861 during the Civil War, then was fully readmitted in 1870. Texas, are you staying?

1882 **The first Labor Day, a national holiday honoring American workers, is celebrated with a parade in New York City.** It now takes place on the first Monday in September, and while it is usually a fun barbecue day, the bummer is that it now marks the unofficial end of summer.

1885 Fill 'er up! Inventor S.F. Bowser sells his first kerosene pump, which later evolves into the drive-up gas pump we know today.

SEPTEMBER 6

1901 The 25th president of the United States, William McKinley, is shot by anarchist Leon Czolgosz at the Pan-American Exposition in Buffalo, New York, and dies several days later. He is one of four U.S. presidents who were assassinated while in office. Abraham Lincoln, James Garfield, and John F. Kennedy were also gunned down while serving their nation. Presidents Ronald Reagan and Theodore Roosevelt both survived gunshots from would-be assassins, and 11 others had close calls.

1915 The first tank, called Little Willie, rolls off the assembly line in England. Little Willie was anything but little. It weighed 16 tons! Willie was not an immediate success—it easily got stuck in trenches and moved at a measly 2 mph— but innovations were quickly made, and tanks transformed the way battles were fought.

1916 "Attention, shoppers!" **The first supermarket, called the Piggly Wiggly, opens in Memphis.** Today, the Piggly Wiggly chain continues to wiggle with nearly 500 locations.

1776 During the American Revolutionary War, *Turtle*, an eight-foot-long wooden submarine, is used to attach a mine to a British ship in New York Harbor. The mission failed when the bomb fell off the ship and harmlessly exploded underwater, but the event marked the first use of a sub in warfare.

1813 **The United States gets an uncle— Uncle Sam.** You may have seen the famous poster of Uncle Sam pointing and asking citizens to join the U.S. Army, but he's not just a cartoon character, he is a real guy. Samuel Wilson was a beef supplier for the army during the War of 1812. According to one version of the story, the barrels he shipped the meat in were stamped "U.S." for "United States," but soldiers started calling the food inside "Uncle Sam's." The nickname stuck, and he became a national icon.

1940 Known as the Blitz, eight dreadful months of bombing begin in London. Germany's air force, the Luftwaffe, continually attacked the city hoping to destroy its infrastructure and its citizens' morale to lead to a quick surrender. But the bombings had the opposite effect on Londoners. While deadly and devastating, the onslaught united the nation with a call to "keep calm and carry on" with their daily lives.

1979 **ESPN (which stands for Entertainment and Sports Programming Network) launches the first 24-hour sports channel.** Back in the day, the founders of the now-multibillion-dollar enterprise built their headquarters on a garbage dump to save money. Makes sense— there sure is a lot of trash talk in sports!

SEPTEMBER 8

1966 • **The TV show *Star Trek* premieres on NBC.**
It became known for combining real-world issues (like racial and class inequality) with sci-fi adventure. Here's the out-of-this-world part—much of the futuristic technology that the show's writers imagined has since been invented and is used today, like Bluetooth communication devices, digital voice assistants like Alexa, and interactive video screens.

2020 • Want some more real-life sci-fi fun? A working lightsaber was created by Canada's Hacksmith Industries. (Hopefully there are no working Darth Vaders walking around up north as well!)

SEPTEMBER 9

1945 • The world's first computer bug is detected and it is an actual bug! A team of scientists at Harvard noticed that their computer, the Mark II, was making consistent errors. When they examined the computer's internal hardware, they found a moth trapped inside that was messing up the path of the electronics. The term bug is now used to describe any kind of glitch in a computer program.

1956 • **Elvis Presley appears for the first time on the super popular *Ed Sullivan Show*.** More than 60 million people tune in to watch him perform, skyrocketing the star to legendary status. Even though Elvis was one of the biggest celebrities in history, he still served when he was drafted into the U.S. Army in 1957 and eventually earned the rank of sergeant.

1846 • Inventor Elias Howe is given a patent for his sewing machine. He must have been a funny guy because he had everyone in stitches. (Sorry, we couldn't resist.)

1946 • While on a train trip in India, Catholic nun **Mother Teresa** has an experience that changes her life—and thousands of others. She later said God spoke to her and instructed, "I was to leave the convent and help the poor while living among them." Mother Teresa dedicated her life to helping disadvantaged people. She was given many awards over her lifetime, including the Nobel Peace Prize, and after her death, she was officially declared a saint by the Catholic Church.

1963 • Writer Stan Lee and artist Jack Kirby publish *X-Men* #1. The first adventure features Professor X, Cyclops, Angel, Beast, and Iceman. (Wolverine didn't pop his claws into the Marvel Universe until 1974.) On creating this new team of heroes, Stan Lee admitted he was inspired partly out of laziness. He was so tired of coming up with origin stories for how his characters got their powers (e.g., bitten by a radioactive spider) that he decided to make them mutants who were simply just born that way.

SEPTEMBER 11

2001

On this morning, 19 terrorists from the group al Qaeda hijack four airplanes and carry out suicide attacks against targets in the United States. Two of the planes were flown into the World Trade Center's Twin Towers, another plane hit the Pentagon in Arlington, Virginia, and a fourth plane crashed in a field in Shanksville, Pennsylvania, after the passengers and crew fought to regain control from the hijackers. Almost 3,000 innocent people died on this terrible day that is referred to as 9/11.

490 BCE • Legend has it that a Greek runner named Pheidippides ran 26.2 miles from Marathon to Athens to deliver the great news that the Greeks had defeated the Persians in battle. The not-so-great news? Poor Pheidippides is said to have dropped dead after giving the message.

1940 • **Four teenagers out hiking in France stumble upon a collection of prehistoric cave paintings.** The Lascaux cave paintings are 15,000 to 17,000 years old and show common animals like horses, deer, and cats, as well as what appears to be a bird-headed man. Let's hope that wasn't common back then!

★ It's National Video Games Day!

The first video game on record is a simple tennis game made in 1958 by physicist William Higinbotham. A lot like the 1970s video game Pong, Tennis for Two was created to attract visitors to see the work being done at Brookhaven National Laboratory on Long Island, New York. It's unclear how interested visitors were in the science presentations but they lined up for hours to play Higinbotham's game.

1958 • The Supreme Court orders the all-white Central High School in Little Rock, Arkansas, to integrate and allow students of all racial backgrounds to attend.

1992 • Flying aboard the space shuttle *Endeavor*, astronaut Mae Jemison becomes the first Black woman to go into space.

SEPTEMBER 13

1848 On this day, an explosion blasted a metal rod straight through the head of railroad worker Phineas Gage. He miraculously survived and maintained all his motor functions, but friends and family say that the accident completely changed his personality. His skull with the hole in it and the rod are now on display at Harvard Medical School's Warren Anatomical Museum. (We don't recommend viewing it right before lunch.)

1916 Roald Dahl, the British author of classics like *Charlie and the Chocolate Factory, James and the Giant Peach* and *Matilda*, is born. During World War II, Dahl served as a fighter pilot and was shot down over the Libyan Desert. After receiving lifesaving surgery, he saved a removed piece of his femur and used it as a paperweight. If you couldn't tell from his books, Dahl had a pretty twisted view on life.

1969 Cartoon villains, you are about to meet your match. **Scooby-Doo, Where Are You! debuts on CBS.** Scooby is a big lovable dog who helps his human pals solve spooky mysteries—while eating as many Scooby Snacks as he can get his paws on.

2016 Conservationists in Cambodia make a huge effort to move 200 royal turtles to a breeding and conservation center. The river-based royal turtle is Cambodia's national reptile and was on the verge of extinction. In 2022, 51 were released back into the wild.

SEPTEMBER 14

1814 Francis Scott Key writes the poem "Defence of Fort M'Henry" while watching the fort getting bombarded by more than 1,500 cannonballs, shells, and rockets fired from British ships during the War of 1812. The poem later became the lyrics to "The Star-Spangled Banner."

1939 Going up! The VS-300, the first successful helicopter to use the main and tail rotor design we know today, lifts off from Stratford, Connecticut.

1959 The USSR spacecraft *Luna 2* crashes into the moon, making it the first man-made object to touch its surface. (Don't worry, there was no one on board.)

2019 **Thieves steal a gold toilet bowl (valued at $6 million) from Blenheim Palace in the U.K.** that was once home to Winston Churchill. That place must have had pretty crappy security.

2020 Astronomers announce that they have detected phosphine, a gas associated with organic things, in the atmosphere of Venus. This hints that we could have living (and gassy) neighbors in our solar system!

★ It's National Hispanic Heritage Month!

From September 15 to October 15, this time period honors the people and cultures of Americans with ancestors from Mexico, the Caribbean, Spain, and Central and South America—and celebrates their major accomplishments. It also pays tribute to the independence of Mexico and several Central American nations.

1776 • **HMS *Beagle*, with naturalist Charles Darwin on board, drops anchor just off the Galapagos Islands.** Darwin's observations of birds and tortoises inform his groundbreaking work *On the Origin of Species*, which describes the theory of evolution and natural selection.

The Theory of Evolution in Simple Terms

Animals within a species aren't all exactly the same. Some have traits that help them survive and thrive (such as a longer neck that can reach higher leaves or the ability to run really fast). They pass those traits on to their offspring, and over time, the characteristics that help survival become more common, and the species gradually changes, or evolves.

1971 • A group of enviromentally focused people board an old wooden boat named *Phyllis Cormack*, attach a "Greenpeace" banner across its bridge, then head off to stop the U.S. military from detonating a nuclear weapon at a remote test site in Alaska. While their mission was unsuccessful, it began a global movement to stop ecological destruction at the hands of humans.

1978 • **Boxer Muhammad Ali defeats Leon Spinks to become the world heavyweight champion for the third time in his career—and is the first fighter to do so.** Ali was famous for his way with his fist as well as his words, spouting gems like, "I float like a butterfly, sting like a bee!"

1983 • *"Achoo, achoo, achoo, ach*...I'm done." British resident Donna Griffiths finally stops sneezing after doing it for two years and 246 days straight. She holds the record for the most sneezes. Which of her friends holds the record for the most *bless you's*?

2021 • SpaceX's *Inspiration4* flight is chartered by billionaire Jared Isaacman and is the first orbital mission with no professional astronauts on board. Would you want to fly in a spaceship with no driver?

FLOAT like

STING like

SEPTEMBER 16

❓ Did You Know?

Pilgrims didn't actually have buckles on their hats and shoes. Buckles were very expensive and considered showy and didn't become fashionable until decades after they left England.

1620 The *Mayflower* leaves England for the New World with 102 Pilgrims and about 30 crew members on board. Originally targeting Virginia, the ship was blown off course by storms and rough seas and landed 500 miles north in Massachusetts instead. After a harsh first year, during which many died, the Pilgrims' colony began to flourish as they made treaties with local Native American tribes and learned from them too. Famously, Governor William Bradford invited the tribes to Plymouth to celebrate the Pilgrims' successful harvest, marking the first Thanksgiving.

1932 The great humanitarian and proponent of nonviolent protests **Mohandas Gandhi begins a hunger strike** from his jail cell to protest British attempts to divide Indian nationalists by treating the so-called untouchables (Dalits) as a separate political class. This was just one of the times Gandhi staged a hunger strike to push to improve the lives of the Dalits and protest violence.

SUGARHILL GANG

1979 **"Rapper's Delight" by the Sugarhill Gang is released** and is the first rap song to become a mainstream radio hit. It immortalizes the phrase, "Now what you hear is not a test, I'm rappin' to the beat/ And me, the groove and my friends are gonna try to move your feet."

SEPTEMBER 17

1787 After Benjamin Franklin gives an impassioned speech about our young nation needing the formal framework of a government, members of the Constitutional Convention in Philadelphia finally stop arguing and sign the final draft of the U.S. Constitution.

1916 World War I flying ace the Red Baron of the German air force wins his first air-to-air combat encounter, known as a dogfight, over France. He went on to win 80 confirmed battles before he was killed in combat on April 21, 1918.

SEPTEMBER 18

1960 In Rome, the first international Paralympic Games were held, where athletes who suffered from spinal cord injuries and other disabilities competed in archery, basketball, fencing, swimming, and table tennis, among other sports. The games continue to be held and hosted in the same city as the Olympic Games.

1998 The release of the movie *Rush Hour* cements kung fu legend Jackie Chan as one of the most exciting and bankable stars in Hollywood. Despite having broken 20-plus bones during his career, Chan insists on doing his own stunts and fight scenes.

SEPTEMBER 19

It's Talk Like a Pirate Day!

What's a pirate's favorite letter?
Rrrrrrrr!

1893 New Zealand becomes the first country to guarantee women the right to vote.

FIRST COMMENT.

2011 Yankees pitcher Mariano Rivera gets his record-setting 602nd career save against the Twins. When he retired in 2013, the Panama-born superstar had 652 saves. He is considered the greatest relief pitcher ever to play the game.

153

SEPTEMBER 20

1519 Portuguese navigator Ferdinand Magellan sets off on the first circumnavigation of the globe. One o the ships in his command completed the trip, but Magellan did not, killed when hit by a poison arrow during a skirmish in what is now the Philippines.

1973 **In a tennis match dubbed the "Battle of the Sexes," top women's player Billie Jean King battles the former number one men's player, Bobby Riggs, and wins.** Riggs had proclaimed that women were not as athletic as men and could not handle pressure. He was very wrong on both counts.

SEPTEMBER 21

1780 During the Revolutionary War, American General Benedict Arnold colludes with British Major John Andre to hand over West Point to the British army. In exchange for the treasonous act, Arnold was promised money and a high rank in the British army. When the plot was discovered, Arnold switched to the British side of the war and eventually escaped to England. The name Benedict Arnold is now used as a term that means traitor.

1912 **World-famous escape artist Harry Houdini debuts his Chinese Water Torture Cell stunt** at the Circus Busch in Berlin, Germany. The trick involved Houdini being lowered upside down into a big tank of water with his feet locked up in heavy stocks. A curtain was drawn in front of the tank, and after several minutes of him—and the audience— holding their breath, he emerged safely. And soggy.

1692 ● **Seven women and one man are hanged for the crime of witchcraft and are the last to be sentenced to death during the Salem Witch Trials.** The trials began in 1692 after several girls in the colonial village of Salem, Massachusetts, started behaving oddly: twitching, barking, and complaining that they felt like they were being pricked by invisible pins. The girls blamed it on local women who they claimed were tormenting them through "the dark arts." Over the next year, more than 200 people were accused of being witches. The trials usually involved a lot of hearsay and no physical evidence. Nineteen supposed witches were hanged, and six others died by other horrible means before the new royal governor of Massachusetts Bay Province, William Phips, brought an end to the trials and released all those still in prison on witchcraft charges.

HOW TO SPOT A WITCH

✓ HOUSE MADE of CANDY

✓ BROOM as TRANSPORTATION

✓ COOKS in a CAULDRON

1994 ● ***Friends* debuts on NBC,** starring Jennifer Aniston, Courteney Cox, Lisa Kudrow, Matt LeBlanc, Matthew Perry, and David Schwimmer, as a group of, well, friends living in New York City. Fans of the show like to take selfies in front of the Central Park Cherry Hill fountain where the opening credits were filmed, but there's one small problem: the fountain that the friends jump around in is actually located on a studio lot in California.

SEPTEMBER

1875 • William Henry McCarty is arrested for stealing a basket of laundry. And it wouldn't be the last time he would break the law. William, better known as Billy the Kid, broke out of jail and became a legendary outlaw in the American West, stealing cattle and horses, gambling, and murdering at least 21 people who got in his way. He was eventually gunned down in New Mexico after making a jailbreak in 1881.

1889 • Long, long, long before video games with funny little Italian guys named Mario and Luigi running around, Nintendo is founded as a playing card company.

2018 • **The first International Day of Sign Languages is observed by the United Nations,** celebrating and calling attention to deaf communities around the world.

1789

The highest court in the land, the Supreme Court, is established. It was originally set up with six justices (we have nine today); all members sign on to serve until death or retirement.

What Is the Supreme Court?

The U.S. government is divided into three branches: executive (the president), legislative (congress), and judicial (federal courts). Supreme Court justices use the Constitution to guide their decisions on cases that have a big impact on American life, including ones involving disputes over free speech and equal rights.

1869

When you hear "Black Friday" you probably think of the day after Thanksgiving when people run to the store at 4 a.m. to get great deals on video game systems and things like that. But the original Black Friday wasn't a good deal at all. Sketchy financier Jay Gould and railroad big shot James Fisk tried to pull off a scheme to drive up the price of gold (and get even more rich in the process). But when the government caught on to their plan, President Ulysses S. Grant ordered massive amounts of gold to be sold to stop gold prices from rising. Grant's order worked a little too well. On this day, gold prices plummeted, the stock market crashed, people panicked, and the nation's economy was damaged for years to come.

1906

President Theodore Roosevelt declares Devils Tower as the first national monument in America. This ensures that the natural rock formation in Wyoming and the surrounding area are protected from development and preserved for future generations to enjoy. There are now 129 national monuments in America and its territories. They are a diverse mix of natural wonders like Devils Tower and historical sites like the Old Soldiers' Home, whose grounds include the cottage where Abraham Lincoln wrote the Emancipation Proclamation.

DEVILS TOWER

1936

Happy birthday to Jim Henson, a guy whose hand did the talking for some of the most famous characters on TV. Wait, what? Jim Henson was the creative genius who invented the Muppets and many of the most memorable characters from *Sesame Street*. Jim was voice and puppeteer of Kermit the Frog, Ernie, Rowlf the Dog, and the Swedish Chef, among many other funny fuzzy icons, and he also sang the nonsense classic "Mah Na Mah Na." (Good luck getting that song out of your head.)

SEPTEMBER 25

1956 • **The first international call is made via a transatlantic phone cable system:** It is a three-way conversation between New York, Ottawa, and London. Prior to this cable, talking overseas involved radio-based service that was not very clear and incredibly expensive. The first word spoken from London during this historic conversation? "Hello."

1981 • **Sandra Day O'Connor is sworn in as the first female U.S. Supreme Court justice** and serves for nearly 25 years.

2020 • Magawa, an African pouched rat, is awarded a gold medal for "lifesaving bravery and devotion" after sniffing out 39 landmines and 28 unexploded bombs in Cambodia. There are an estimated 5 million landmines still buried throughout the country, and people (and rats) are doing everything they can to clear them to prevent devastating injuries.

SEPTEMBER 26

1960 • **The first televised presidential debate hits the airwaves, pitting John F. Kennedy against Richard Nixon.** Many believe that Kennedy's comfort in front of the camera and Nixon's decision not to wear any TV makeup (and the fact that he was sweating bullets) in this first of four debates helped Kennedy edge out a win in one of the closest elections in U.S. history.

2008 • Former Swiss fighter pilot Yves Rossy finds an inventive way to cross the English Channel: He uses a jet-propelled wing strapped to his back. The flight took only nine and a half minutes, which is faster than taking a train through the Chunnel, but it did require a parachute, so maybe not as convenient.

2009 • Lots of people say that plastic is bad for the environment, but the town of Bundanoon in Australia takes a major step to do something about it: They enact a voluntary ban on the sale of bottled water—unless it is a reusable bottle. Cheers to that!

1908 ● **The first Model T is assembled at the Ford Piquette Plant in Detroit.**

Why Was the Model-T So Important?

The Model T automobile was affordable, simple to operate, and Henry Ford's innovative approach to utilizing an assembly line meant that it could be mass-produced. All those things came together to make the Model T one of the most popular cars in history. From 1908 to 1927, 15 million cars (nicknamed Tin Lizzies) helped Americans hit the road.

fig. 1
THE FIRST BACK-SEAT DRIVER

WOOF

1922 ● Way before *Avatar*, the first 3D movie, called *The Power of Love*, is screened. It features knife fights, robberies, and, as you might have guessed from the title, *love*. We would suggest you check it out, but the 3D version—shown only twice—has been lost.

2022 ● **NASA aims the *DART* spacecraft at a distant asteroid and makes a direct hit, successfully changing its flight path.** Why? We don't want to freak you out, but we live in a very crowded universe, and some day (not anytime soon) we could have a big problem if a big asteroid got on a collision course with earth. Luckily, the heroes at NASA proved we don't have to just be sitting ducks. So go ahead and give us your biggest, baddest asteroid, universe, we're ready! (Actually, please don't.)

BULLSEYE!

DART

SEPTEMBER 28

551
● **It's the birthday of Chinese philosopher and teacher Confucius,** who was known for thought-provoking sayings like, "Forget injuries, never forget kindnesses."

1066
● William the Conqueror invades England from France with 7,000 troops. After winning the Battle of Hastings, he became the first Norman king of England. Oddly enough, the king of England didn't speak English!

1920
● In one of the most shocking cheating scandals in professional sports, **eight Chicago White Sox baseball players are indicted by a grand jury for intentionally losing the World Series.** They did it in exchange for $100,000 from gangsters who planned on betting big for the Sox's opponents, the Cincinnati Reds, to win. Dubbed the Black Sox Scandal, all the players involved were banned from baseball for life, even those who claimed that their lives were threatened by the gangsters if they didn't go along with the scheme.

1928
● A big mess becomes a big discovery. Scottish scientist **Alexander Fleming finds that mold has started growing on a petri dish he left uncovered next to a window.** Peeking closer, he realizes that the mold seems to be killing the harmful bacteria he was examining. He was able to harvest the "mold juice," which would later be called penicillin, the world's first antibiotic.

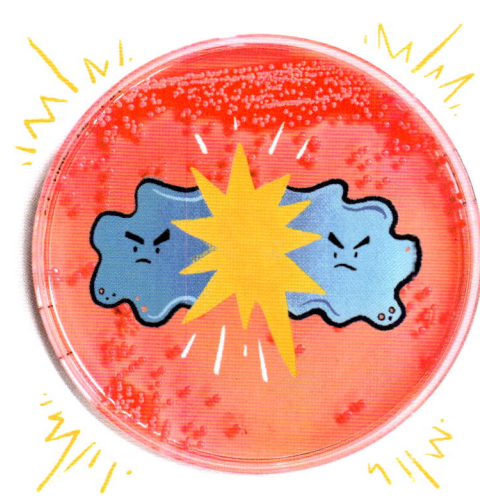

1969
● A very, very old rock lands in Murchison, Australia. Analysis decades later reveals that the Murchison meteorite contains the oldest material ever found—stardust that is billions of years older than our solar system.

1829 • **Sir Robert Peel establishes England's first professional police force, the Metropolitan Police (better known as Scotland Yard).** It became the model of how police forces operate throughout the world, including regular foot patrols and undercover cops mixing in with bad guys to make busts.

1916 • *Ka-ching!* Oil tycoon John D. Rockefeller becomes the world's first billionaire. Today there are more than 3,000 billionaires, but no one has broken the trillionaire mark yet. Maybe it'll be you! (P.S. If it is you, can we borrow five bucks?)

OFFICIAL UNIFORM

SEPTEMBER 30

1868 • The wildly successful book *Little Women* is published in America—but its author didn't actually want to write it. When Louisa May Alcott was approached by her publisher to "write a book for girls," she said she wasn't interested. But then she started thinking about her unique childhood, and the wheels started turning. Alcott wrote in her diary that her and her sisters' "plays and experiences may prove interesting though I doubt it." She was wrong. *Little Women* became an instant classic and has been enjoyed by generations and generations of readers. (Are you a Meg, Jo, Beth, or Amy?)

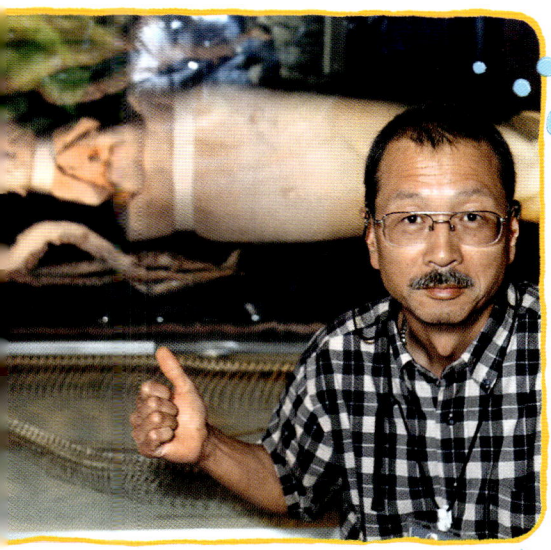

1960 • The cartoon *The Flintstones*, about life in the suburbs of prehistoric America, premieres. While it wasn't exactly factually accurate (cavemen and women did not use water squirted out of a woolly mammoth trunk as a dishwasher), it did pave the way for great cartoon family shows like *The Simpsons* and *Family Guy*.

2004 • **Japanese researchers lure a giant squid with bait and capture the first images of the incredible invertebrate in its deep-ocean home.** The feat is impressive since the creatures, which can grow to be longer than 40 feet, are hard to find in their natural habitat.

THIS DAY IN *my* HISTORY
SEPTEMBER

Fill in any memorable events from your life here.

1 ....

2 ....

3 ....

4 ....

5 ....

6 ....

7 ....

8 ....

9 ....

10 ....

11 ....

12 ....

13 ....

14 ....

15 ....

16 ....

17 ....

18 ....

19 ....

20 ....

21 ....

22 ....

23 ....

24 ....

25 ....

26 ....

27 ....

28 ....

29 ....

30 ....

OCTOBER 1

1903
- The first baseball World Series game is played, with the Pittsburgh Pirates beating the Boston Americans 7-3. Lucky for Boston, it was a best-of-nine series, and despite that first loss, they took home the first title.

1971
- Obsessed with the idea of being able to use cosmic rays to look for hidden areas and treasures within Egyptian pyramids, **British engineer Godfrey Hounsfield invents a way to look inside the most treasured place on earth: the human skull.** His invention, the CT scan, allows doctors to take 3D images of the brain, opening new possibilities for medical care and treatment.

1988
- **Steffi Graf beats Gabriela Sabatini to win the women's singles tennis gold medal at the Seoul Olympics**—clinching the first and only Golden Slam in history. She earned the Golden Slam by winning the Australian Open, French Open, Wimbledon, U.S. Open, and the Olympic gold medal all in one year! This is considered one of the greatest seasons of tennis ever played.

OCTOBER 2

1608 • Dutch inventor Hans Lippershey files a patent for an instrument that can be used "for seeing things far away as if they were near." This instrument, the telescope, transformed the world (well, the universe) of astronomy.

1925 • **American entertainer and dancer Josephine Baker performs her _La Revue Nègre_ for the first time in Paris.** As a teen, she escaped poverty and discrimination in the United States and moved to France, where she became one of the most famous performers in the world.

1950 • The first _Peanuts_ cartoon strip by Charles Schultz runs in seven newspapers. Charlie Brown, Snoopy, and the rest of the gang would go on to be featured in movies, TV specials, and even outer space. A Snoopy doll rode aboard the space shuttle _Columbia_ in 1990. Good grief!

1959 • **Sometimes futuristic, sometimes scary, and always freaky, _The Twilight Zone_ premieres on TV.** The show, created by Rod Serling, takes viewers on fantastic and sometimes upsetting journeys that always have weird plot twists. For instance, in one episode, aliens come to earth and in no time at all solve all of humanity's problems. Then they invite everyone to board their ship, holding up a book entitled _To Serve Man_. People happily file onto the ship, but as one scientist realizes too late, the book isn't a manual for helping mankind, it is a cookbook. The aliens are literally going to serve man—for dinner!

OCTOBER 3

1942 • Turn your old keys into tanks! **The U.S. government begins "scrap days,"** asking every American to donate any metal that could be melted down and used as raw materials for weapons and supplies for the armed forces in World War II.

1990 • After 45 years of separation, East and West Germany are reunited as the Federal Republic of Germany. Coincidentally, it was on this same day in 1964 that a group of West German students successfully helped many people stuck in East Berlin make a daring escape. They dug a secret tunnel under the Berlin Wall, which was later named Tunnel 57, because 57 people escaped through it over the course of two nights before it was discovered and demolished by East German watch guards.

OCTOBER 4

1883 • The Orient Express, a super luxurious train, begins its first official journey from Paris to Istanbul, Turkey, with 40 passengers on board. A ticket cost about one-fourth of an average Frenchman's annual salary in the 1880s—luxury did not come cheaply!

1927 • The dusty, explode-y work of carving Mount Rushmore begins. The idea came from South Dakota historian Doane Robinson as a way to attract tourists to the state. Under the supervision of sculptor Gutzon Borglum, nearly 400 workers—both men and women—took 14 years, and lots of dynamite, to complete the remarkable monument depicting the faces of Presidents George Washington, Thomas Jefferson, Abraham Lincoln, and Theodore Roosevelt.

1957 • The Soviet Union kicks off the space age with its launch of *Sputnik*, the world's first artificial satellite. Amateur radio operators in America could hear *Sputnik* beeping as it passed over the country several times a day, astonishing and scaring them.

2022 • Yankees right fielder Aaron Judge hits his 62nd home run, breaking Roger Maris's American League single-season home run record. The ball was caught by a fan in the stands of Globe Life Field in Texas and was later auctioned off for $1.5 million. Great hit—and an even greater catch!

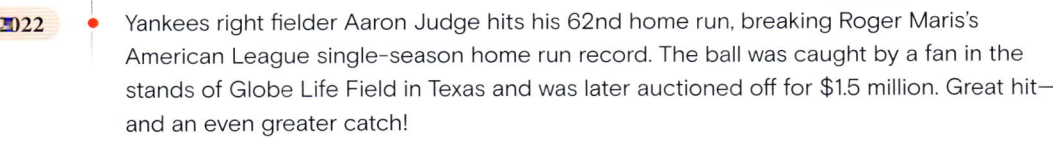

⭐ **It's National Taco Day!**

According to historian Jeffrey M. Pilcher, tacos were invented in the 18th century by silver miners in Mexico. They were called tacos because *taco* was the name of a type of explosive the miners used, which were folded-up pieces of paper stuffed with gunpowder and then jammed into holes in the rock. (Note: Don't eat one of those tacos unless you want to have really, really, *really* bad heartburn.)

OCTOBER 5

1970 · It's a beautiful day in the TV neighborhood. **PBS, home to educational and fun shows like *Sesame Street* and *Mister Rogers' Neighborhood*, begins broadcasting.**

2006 · Scientists announce the discovery of the complete skeleton of a plesiosaur, a 33-foot-long marine reptile that had teeth the size of cucumbers. Very aptly, they named it the Monster.

2022 · NASA astronaut Nicole Aunapu Mann blasts off on the SpaceX *Falcon*, part of a four-person crew heading to the International Space Station. This historic moment makes her the first Native American woman to launch into space.

OCTOBER 6

1866 · Bad guy brothers John and Simeon Reno pull off the first known train robbery in American history, stealing $13,000 (which is, like, $450,000 in today's money). While trains had been robbed in stations before this, the Reno brothers were the first to stop a train as it was traveling in the middle of nowhere (in this case, Jackson County, Indiana) so that they could go about their thieving business without worrying about nearby law officers or do-gooder citizens interfering.

THEY'LL PAY *for* THIS...

NO GOATS

1945 · **Curse of the Billy Goat!** The Chicago Cubs got ready for a home game against the Detroit Tigers, feeling pretty good about taking a 3-1 lead in the World Series. But then Billy Sianis, the owner of the nearby Billy Goat Tavern, showed up at Wrigley Field and tried to buy a ticket for himself and his pet goat to watch the game. Wrigley's ushers refused to let the goat in, and so a very angry Sianis stormed away proclaiming, "Them Cubs, they ain't gonna win no more!" Sadly for fans, his words became prophecy. Not only did the Cubs lose that series, but they also didn't make it back to the World Series for 71 years! The lesson here? Be nice to goats!

2010 · Instagram launches and instantly racks up 25,000 users in one day. At last count, there are more than 1.2 billion Instagram users on the planet who mostly use the popular technological platform to share pictures of what they're eating for lunch.

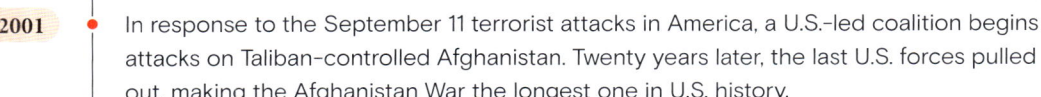

OCTOBER 7

1982 — **The Broadway musical *Cats* debuts.** Depending on how you feel about grown people crawling around and licking themselves as they sing, it is an amazing or terrible thing that the show ran for 18 years.

2001 — In response to the September 11 terrorist attacks in America, a U.S.-led coalition begins attacks on Taliban-controlled Afghanistan. Twenty years later, the last U.S. forces pulled out, making the Afghanistan War the longest one in U.S. history.

2021 — The International 10, an e-sports tournament for the multiplayer video game Dota 2, features the biggest prize pool in history—$40 million!

OCTOBER 8

1871 — A fire, supposedly caused by a cow kicking over a lit lantern in Patrick and Catherine O'Leary's barn, quickly spreads throughout Chicago. The resulting two-day blaze kills hundreds of people, destroys 17,450 buildings, and leaves 100,000 homeless. Added up, the total damage cost about $4 billion in today's money. In 1997, the Chicago City Council officially declared that the O'Learys and their cow were innocent and that a man named Daniel "Peg Leg" Sullivan was likely the cause of the catastrophe.

1945 — Let the fast-popping popcorn begin! On this day, self-educated **inventor Percy Spencer files his patent for the microwave oven.**

2004 — Kenyan environmental justice organizer Wangari Maathai becomes the first African woman to receive the Nobel Peace Prize. She is awarded the prize for her innovative efforts to protect the environment and improve the living and economic conditions of impoverished people at the same time. Her Green Belt Movement has paid rural women to plant 30 million trees throughout the country for over 30 years.

OCTOBER 9

1000 It's Leif Erikson Day, celebrating the first European explorer thought to have set foot in North America.

1887 **Elizabeth Cochrane Seaman, writing under the pen name Nellie Bly, publishes the first article in a series that will become the basis for the book *Ten Days in a Mad-House*.** Nellie went undercover; she checked herself into New York's notorious Blackwell's Island Insane Asylum for Women and reported on the horrible conditions patients faced. Bly went on to become one of the most famous reporters in the world.

OCTOBER 10

1845 Secretary of the Navy George Bancroft founds the U.S. Naval Academy in Annapolis, Maryland. Students there face an incredibly tough four years of academic, military, and physical training and graduate as officers in either the Navy or the Marines. There are a lot of traditions at this academy—some very patriotic and some very weird. An example is the annual challenge to freshmen to climb up to the top of a stone pillar on campus. If that wasn't hard enough, the upper-class students first cover it in thick grease.

1967 **The Outer Space Treaty goes into effect.** It's an agreement between nations that all wars and international tension would be left here on earth and that the exploration of space would be used solely for the benefit of all mankind. No nation could claim control over any celestial bodies (like the moon), and no weapons of mass destruction could be brought to space. In short, space is a place to be nice!

OCTOBER 11

1919 The first airline meal is served on a flight from London to Paris. What was on the menu? Most likely cold fried chicken, fruit salad, and sandwiches, served in wicker baskets. It was basically a picnic in the sky without the ants.

1975 Sketch comedy show *Saturday Night Live* premieres on NBC. A lot of famous funny people got their start here, including Eddie Murphy, Adam Sandler, and Tina Fey. *SNL* is genuinely live...but when controversial comedians host, the show might have a seven-second delay to give the director enough time to bleep out any, um, interesting words the performer might say.

1987 **The AIDS Memorial Quilt is unfolded on the National Mall in Washington, D.C.** Each panel has the name of a person who died during the epidemic and was created by their loved ones. The quilt, which now has more than 50,000 names, toured the nation many times. In 2019, it was returned to the care of the National AIDS Memorial, an organization based in San Francisco, the city where early AIDS activists had first conceived it. The AIDS Quilt is the largest piece of community folk art in the world, the premiere symbol of the AIDS epidemic, and a living memorial for those who died during its height.

OCTOBER 12

1979 The most powerful storm ever recorded, Typhoon Tip, forms over the western Pacific Ocean, with peak sustained winds of 190 mph. It's not just powerful, it's massive. Had the storm formed over the United States, it would have covered Texas to New York.

1990 The first Indigenous People's Day (then called Native American Day) is celebrated in South Dakota. Although it is not an official federal holiday, in 2021, President Biden issued the first presidential proclamation to clarify its meaning, writing, "Today, we recognize Indigenous peoples' resilience and strength as well as the immeasurable positive impact that they have made on every aspect of American society."

❓ Did You Know?

Typhoons and hurricanes are the same kind of storm—a tropical cyclone. They just get different names depending on where they occur.

1 **HURRICANES**
Above the North Atlantic, central North Pacific, or eastern North Pacific Oceans

2 **TYPHOONS**
Above Northwest Pacific Ocean (usually East Asia)

3 **TROPICAL CYCLONES**
South Pacific and Indian Ocean

OCTOBER 13

1792 — **The cornerstone is laid for a presidential residence in America's capital city of Washington, D.C.** In 1800, President John Adams became the first president to live in the home, which was dubbed the White House because of its white-gray stone exterior.

1958 — *A Bear Called Paddington* is first published. Its author, Michael Bond, was inspired to write the story after he spotted a lonely-looking teddy bear sitting on a store shelf on Christmas Eve.

2009 — The first celebration of Ada Lovelace Day, recognizing the achievements of women in STEM. Born in 1815, Lovelace was a mathematician who, alongside Charles Babbage, created a machine that could input data using punch cards. In short: She was the world's first computer programmer even though computers weren't invented yet!

OCTOBER 14

1926 — *Winnie-the-Pooh* **by A.A. Milne is released** in England and the United States on the same day by two different publishers. Pooh becomes one of the most beloved characters of all time, thanks to quotes like, "People say nothing is impossible, but I do nothing every day."

1947 — Air Force Captain Chuck Yeager becomes the first person to fly faster than the speed of sound. His experimental aircraft, the Bell X-1 *Glamorous Glennis*, was air-launched, meaning it dropped out of the bomb bay of a B-29 bomber and then used its rocket engine to climb to its test altitude of 43,000 feet to begin its record-setting run of 700 mph.

2012 — Watch that first step! Millions of YouTube viewers witness Austrian skydiver Felix Baumgartner step off of a specially designed balloon that was hovering on the edge of space. His 24-mile jump broke multiple records, including the highest free fall and the highest manned balloon flight. He also became the first man to break the speed of sound in free fall (he reached 843.6 mph!). And if you watched, you're part of the record too. The 8 million concurrent views were the highest ever on YouTube. Congrats!

OCTOBER 15

1952 • **The children's classic *Charlotte's Web* by E.B. White is published.** If you can read this touching book about a spider named Charlotte who saves her pig friend Wilbur's life without crying, then you are tougher than we are!

1989 • **Wayne Gretzky breaks Gordie Howe's 1,850 career points record, becoming the NHL's all-time top scorer.** (In hockey, a player gets a point for either scoring or assisting in a score.) When he retired, Gretzky held a total of 61 records, including the most career points at 2,857. No wonder his nickname was the Great One.

1997 • The 34-year-old British pilot Andy Green gets behind the wheel of a car and breaks the land speed record, cruising at 763.035 mph. It wasn't just any car, as you might have guessed. The vehicle, the Thrust SSC, was essentially a fighter jet without wings. It was so powerful that when it sped off, a sonic boom knocked paintings off the walls in houses 10 miles away.

OCTOBER 16

1968 • Standing on the 200-meter winners' podium at the Olympics in Mexico City, **American runners Tommie Smith (gold) and John Carlos (bronze) raised their fists in the Black Power salute as the National Anthem played, to protest the racism and injustice Black Americans faced back home.** They were suspended from the Olympic team and forced to leave the Olympic Village because of their peaceful protest. The two men faced many hardships when they got back home—even death threats. Nearly 50 years later, President Barack Obama honored them at a White House ceremony, saying, "Their powerful silent protest in the 1968 Games was controversial, but it woke folks up and created greater opportunity for those that followed."

1997 • Future tennis great Naomi Osaka is born in Japan. Her dad, Leonard Francois (who is from Haiti), and mom, Tamaki Osaka (from Japan), moved their family to New York when she was 3. They soon relocated to Florida so that Naomi could pursue a career in the game. You could say that the plan worked out pretty well: In 2019, she became the first Asian tennis player to be ranked number one in the world in singles.

OCTOBER 17

1931 • Notorious gangster Al "Scarface" Capone is sentenced to 11 years in prison for tax evasion. For years, he was a feared crime boss in Chicago, infamous for his brutality with rivals, landing him on the FBI's 10 Most Wanted list. So how did he get that ominous nickname? When he was 14, he joined a street gang and was cut across the face in a fight. Capone made millions illegally selling alcohol during Prohibition and died at age 48, almost eight years after being released from Alcatraz prison.

2006 • The population of the United States reaches 300 million. (No wonder it is so hard to get tickets to Taylor Swift concerts.)

What Is the Most Populated Country in the World?

For a long time, the answer was China. But in 2023, India surpassed its neighbor. Each country has over 1.4 billion people. So doing some quick math, compared to the United States, that means...there are a lot of people in China and India!

OCTOBER 18

1867 • **The U.S. formally takes possession of Alaska from Russia for $7.2 million** That might sound like a lot, but Alaska is huge (about twice the size of Texas), and so it basically breaks down to paying less than 2 cents per acre. Despite its super low cost, many American politicians were against the purchase—until they found out there was gold and oil there. Score!

1921 • **Breakfast will never be the same thanks to Charles P. Strite, who receives a patent for the electric toaster on this day.** Unfortunately, he didn't patent a fix for burnt toast.

1781 British General Charles Cornwallis and 8,000 troops surrender to General George Washington after being surrounded by some 16,000 American and French troops at Yorktown. This was the last major battle in the Revolutionary War. While fighting continued for some time after, this victory signaled that the colonists won their independence.

1973 Rising tension and conflict in the Middle East lead to an organization of Arab oil-producing countries known as OPEC to refuse to sell oil to the U.S. This began the gas crisis of 1973 to '74. Shortages in fuel caused huge lines at gas stations, customers needing reservations to fill up, businesses shutting off electricity, and some towns going so far as banning Christmas lights so as not to waste energy.

1987 On this day, known as Black Monday, stock markets all around the world crash, causing economic panic. Unlike other crashes, the market soon recovered its losses, and within two years, U.S. stock markets shot above their precrash values.

2015 **Scientists at the University of California announce that they have found signs that life on earth may have started 4.1 billion years ago**, shortly after the earth formed 4.54 billion years ago. (If you can call 440 million years "shortly.")

OCTOBER 20

1947 The Red Scare kicks into high gear: A Congressional committee in the U.S. House of Representatives begins investigating communist influence in Hollywood. Hundreds of actors, writers, and producers are accused of having communist sympathies. Some go to jail after refusing to give more names to the committee; others are blacklisted (prevented from working). In 1954, Senator Joseph McCarthy launches more anti-communist charges, this time aimed at members of the U.S. Armed Forces. Once these investigations were broadcast on TV, citizens were outraged at the abuse of power by McCarthy and the lack of evidence on display. The hearings stopped, and although he kept his job, McCarthy was rendered powerless by his fellow senators.

2020 **Under the waves off the coast of Australia, scientists discover a giant tower of coral that is taller than the Empire State Building.** It's the first time in more than 100 years that a new coral structure has been discovered on the Great Barrier Reef.

OCTOBER 21

❓ **Did You Know?**

Wonder Woman's creator, William Moulton Marston, wasn't just a writer; he was also a psychologist and inventor. He created a device that measured blood pressure that helped lead to the development of the lie detector machine.

1854 • Florence Nightingale and a group of nurses leave England for Constantinople in Turkey to help injured soldiers fighting in the Crimean War. Nightingale's observations and innovations caring for sick and wounded soldiers became the foundation for modern nursing.

1941 • ***All Star Comics*** **#8 features the first appearance of Wonder Woman.** In this origin story, U.S. Army captain Steve Trevor accidentally crashes onto the mysterious Paradise Island. The island's princess, Diana, decides to leave with him to help America fight the Nazis, leaving her riches and the chance of eternal life behind.

OCTOBER 22

1797 • Look out below! André-Jacques Garnerin conducts the first successful parachute jump, floating down from a hot-air balloon over Paris. Leonardo da Vinci was the first to sketch the idea of a parachute, but Garnerin was the first to put it to a life-or-death test. His design was inspired when he was imprisoned in a tower during the French Revolution, and he wondered if he could use a canopy to slow his fall if he tried jumping out a window.

1962 • **The Cuban Missile Crisis occurs.** President John F. Kennedy announces on TV that U.S. spy planes have discovered Soviet missiles in Cuba capable of hitting cities in the United States. Kennedy orders a blockade of Cuba, putting America and the USSR on the brink of war. Thankfully, Kennedy and Soviet leader Nikita Khrushchev were able to come to a peaceful resolution, diffusing what came frighteningly close to nuclear war.

USA

CUBA

1958 • The Smurfs appear for the first time in comics. Creator, writer, and artist Pierre Culliford, who went by the pen name Peyo, put them in his Belgian sword-and-sorcery adventure series called *Johan and Peewit*. He got the name Smurf when he was having dinner with French cartoonist André Franquin, and he couldn't remember the French word for salt, so he just made up a word. Want a little Smurf on your popcorn?

2015 • Singer Adele's single "Hello" is the first song to get more than a million downloads in its first week. When asked by *Time* magazine about her fame, she responded, "It's a bit ridiculous." Is there a record for being the most humble?

2018 • If you want to take a drive with beautiful water views, take **the Hong Kong-Zhuai-Macau Bridge, the longest sea bridge-tunnel system on the planet.** After a decade of construction, the 34.2 mile system of bridges and underwater tunnels opens, connecting Hong Kong to mainland China. Before it opened, driving on land around the waters of the Pearl River Estuary took more than four hours. Now the trip only takes about 45 minutes.

OCTOBER 24

1901 • **Annie Edson Taylor, a 63-year-old schoolteacher, becomes the first person to go over Niagara Falls in a barrel and survive.** (We'd say please don't try this at home, but we're pretty sure you don't have a 325-foot-tall waterfall in your backyard.)

1992 • The Toronto Blue Jays put the "World" in the World Series, beating the Atlanta Braves and becoming the first Major League Baseball team from outside the United States to take home the trophy.

OCTOBER 25

1975 • **Daredevil Evel Knievel jumps over 14 Greyhound buses on a motorcycle**—his longest successful jump in a career filled with dazzling highs and bone-breaking lows.

Who Was Evel Knievel?

Born Robert Craig Knievel Jr., the daredevil stunt rider earned his nickname Evel (pronounced "evil") after getting in trouble with the law. One day, while working at a motorcycle shop, he had a big idea to bring in more customers: He announced he'd make a 40-foot motorcycle jump over parked cars and a box of rattlesnakes. Evel cleared the cars but landed on the rattlesnakes—and the crowd went wild. From there, he built a career on daring (and often unsuccessful) jumps, fearlessly launching himself over the fountain at Caesars Palace in Las Vegas and trying to jump across the Snake River Canyon in a steam-powered vehicle, to name a few. By the time he retired, he was the most famous daredevil in the world, and he received an award no one else on earth would want: the Guinness World Record for the most bones broken in a lifetime—433!

OCTOBER 26

1825 • The 363-mile Erie Canal, which connects the Great Lakes to the Hudson River, officially opens. The waterway's connections made New York City the commercial center of America and encouraged people to expand westward. The original canal was just four feet deep and 40 feet wide and had a towpath on the side, where horses and mules tied to barges would drag thousands of pounds of cargo through the water. As far as jobs go, that sounds like a real drag.

1881 • After silver was discovered in the town of Tombstone, Arizona, it became one of the richest places in the Southwest—which attracted the attention of a lot of bad guys. Lawman Wyatt Earp and his brothers decided to bring law and order to the town, but a group of cowboys and thieves, including the Clantons and McLaurys, wanted control. And so on this day, the two groups battled in a shootout at the O.K. Corral. It lasted all of 30 seconds but became a legendary incident of the old West. Around 30 shots were fired, and when the dust cleared, the Earps were victorious...and thrown in jail for murder until a judge decided that their actions were necessary to preserve peace in Tombstone.

OCTOBER 27

1904 — **The largest underground rail system in the world, New York City's subway, makes its inaugural run.** Every day, millions of New Yorkers use this fast, affordable (and, sure, sometimes very dirty) system's nearly 700 miles of tracks to get to anywhere they need to be in the city's five boroughs.

1925 — New Yorker Fred Waller patents the first water skis. He called them Dolphin Akwa-Skees. Water-skiing had actually been invented a few years earlier by a guy named Ralph Samuelson, who used boards from a barrel. Samuelson never patented it, so he didn't get rich, but he did become famous performing and teaching water-ski tricks all around the country. (Specifically, the parts of the country that had water.)

OCTOBER 28

1904 — St. Louis police officially adopt a new method of investigation: fingerprints. We're going to guess that it was also on this day that criminals started buying (or stealing) a lot more gloves.

1919 — The Volstead Act passes in U.S. Congress, establishing Prohibition.

1965 — Construction is completed on the Gateway Arch, a 630-foot-high curved stainless-steel structure in St. Louis. Visitors aren't allowed to climb its 1,076 steps but can take a four-minute tram ride up to its observation deck. (Honestly, we'd take the tram even if we were allowed to walk up all those stairs!)

What Was Prohibition?

The 18th Amendment began Prohibition, which banned making, transporting, and selling alcohol within the United States. While the stated goal was to improve the health and wellness of citizens, the main result was a lot of crime. Alcohol was made, transported, and sold illegally by bootleggers, and secret bars known as speakeasies popped up everywhere. All this illicit activity led to a rise in gang violence and organized crime. Pressure from the public and business owners to bring legal alcohol back led to the 21st Amendment in 1933, which repealed the 18th and ended Prohibition.

★ It's National First Responders Day!

This day honors and gives thanks to the men and women in police and fire departments and to the EMTs, paramedics, and others who bravely put their lives on the line to keep us all safe when emergencies strike.

OCTOBER 29

1929 It's Black Tuesday. A massive stock market crash wipes out billions of dollars, leading to the Great Depression in America. At the worst point in this terrible 10-year period, 15 million Americans were unemployed, and nearly half the country's banks collapsed, vaporizing people's life savings in an instant.

1998 At the age of 77, nearly four decades after he became the first American to orbit the earth, John Glenn goes back into space aboard the space shuttle *Discovery*. At the time, he was the oldest human to travel in space—and during the shuttle's nine-day mission, he helped with a NASA study on health and aging.

2012 Superstorm Sandy hits the East Coast of the United States, causing devastation in 24 states. Although the storm was downgraded from a hurricane, it caused massive flooding and power outages in New York and New Jersey that left people in emergency conditions for weeks.

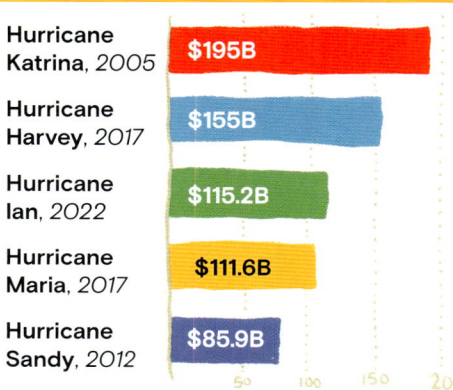

The Cost of the Most Devastating Storms in the U.S.

Hurricane **Katrina**, 2005	$195B
Hurricane **Harvey**, 2017	$155B
Hurricane **Ian**, 2022	$115.2B
Hurricane **Maria**, 2017	$111.6B
Hurricane **Sandy**, 2012	$85.9B

50   100   150   200

OCTOBER 30

1937 **Writer and director Orson Welles and his Mercury Theatre on the Air group perform a live radio play of H.G. Wells' *The War of the Worlds***, a sci-fi novel about a deadly Martian invasion of New Jersey. Giving it a new twist, the script for the play took the story of the novel and changed it into realistic-sounding news reports. It was a little too realistic, and many listeners across the country panicked, calling local police and begging for protection from the invading Martians. Welles said he and the other creators had no intention of fooling the public and honestly believed the story was too silly for anyone to take seriously. (Plus, anyone paying attention might have noticed it was the exact same plot as a very famous novel.)

2003 Just a few months out of high school, LeBron James made his NBA debut with the Cleveland Cavaliers. Although the Cavs lost the game, LeBron gave viewers a taste of what was to come, scoring 25 points, grabbing six rebounds, and dealing nine assists during the game. Many argue whether he or Michael Jordan is the GOAT (Greatest of All Time). But there's no debate about this: With four NBA Championship rings and four MVP awards, LeBron James is very, very good at basketball!

1517 • **Monk and theologian Martin Luther posts his "Ninety-five Theses,"** a manifesto about a scandal within the Catholic Church, on the door of a church in Germany. The manifesto was then copied and circulated and helped lead to the Reformation, which created a new branch of Christianity called Protestantism.

1950 • It's the first trick or treat for UNICEF. Pennsylvania minister Clyde Allison, his wife, Mary Emma, and their children began collecting change to help hungry children badly affected by World War II and collaborated with UNICEF to make it a national effort. Since then, the program has raised $195 million to buy food and vaccines for needy children around the world.

How Did Halloween Start?

Why do we get dressed in crazy costumes and hang skeletons up in our windows for Halloween? It all started with the ancient Celtic festival of Samhain, during which worshippers lit bonfires and wore costumes to scare away ghosts. Then in the eighth century, Pope Gregory III declared November 1 as All Saints Day, which used some of the same traditions as Samhain. The night before that was known as All Hallows Eve, which became Halloween. The celebrations kept evolving over the years, resulting in the greatest holiday custom of all-time: people giving out full-size candy bars to trick-or-treaters!

THIS DAY IN *my* HISTORY
OCTOBER

Fill in any memorable events from your life here.

1 ....

2 ....

3 ....

4 ....

5 ....

6 ....

7 ....

8 ....

9 ....

10 ....

11 ....

12 ....

13 ....

14 ....

15 ....

16 ....

17 ....

18 ....

19 ....

20 ....

21 ....

22 ....

23 ....

24 ....

25 ....

26 ....

27 ....

28 ....

29 ....

30 ....

31 ....

NOVEMBER 1

T'S NATIVE AMERICAN HERITAGE MONTH! In 1990, President George H.W. Bush designated November as the month to celebrate the incredible contributions that the first Americans have made to the establishment and growth of the United States.

10 Native American Inventions That We Use Today

1. Baby bottles
2. Cable suspension bridges
3. Hammocks
4. Kayaks
5. Mouthwash
6. Raised-bed gardens
7. Rubber
8. Snow goggles
9. Syringes
10. Topical pain relievers

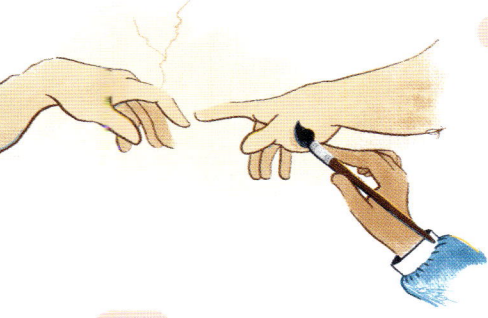

1512 • **Members of the public are allowed to view the ceiling of the Sistine Chapel in the Vatican for the first time.** The ceiling, painted by Michelangelo with scenes from the Bible, is considered one of the greatest works of art ever created. It took four years to complete, with the artist standing or lying on top of a 20-foot-tall scaffolding to reach the ceiling. (Guess a 20-foot-long paintbrush would be a little hard to hold.)

1974 • Artist Yuko Shimizu creates a cute new character named Hello Kitty for the Japanese merchandising company Sanrio. Did you know that even though she appears to have whiskers and a tail, Hello Kitty's official biography explains that she is a girl, not a cat?

2012 • **Astronomers detect light from the universe's first stars**, which formed right after the big bang occurred, about 13.7 billion years ago.

What Is the Big Bang?

It is a universally accepted theory that the universe started as an incredibly hot and dense single point that exploded—bang!—then rapidly expanded, forming all the stars, gasses, rocks, moons, and planets. (That includes the one we are sitting on right now, reading this book.)

NOVEMBER **2**

1947 The Hughes Flying Boat is piloted over Long Beach Harbor in California by eccentric millionaire Howard Hughes on its first and only flight. The largest aircraft ever built at the time, it had a wingspan longer than a football field, was powered by eight massive propeller engines, and had enough room inside to transport more than 700 soldiers. The plane was made of laminated birch and spruce wood, earning it the nickname the Spruce Goose. On that first test flight, the massive craft was able to lift off, flying 70 feet above the water for a mile before landing. The prototype worked, but it never went into production, much to the relief of all of the birch trees in the area.

1898 Here's something to cheer about: Johnny Campbell leads the crowd encouraging the University of Minnesota football team, inventing cheerleading in America.

1983 President Ronald Reagan signs legislation that designates Martin Luther King Jr. Day as an annual federal holiday. The day is meant for all Americans to honor the civil rights leader by doing volunteer work in our communities.

2020 **"Baby Shark" becomes the most-watched video on YouTube** with more than 7.04 billion views. "Most-viewed shark, doo-doo, doo-doo, doo-doo!"

Now she says she wants to become an influencer...

NOVEMBER **3**

🕐 Did You Know?

The Freedom Tower, which is the tallest building in the United States, is exactly 1,776 feet tall, referring to the year 1776 when the Declaration of Independence was approved by the United States Continental Congress.

1957 The first living creature to go into orbit around the earth is a dog named Laika, who blasted off aboard the Soviet spacecraft *Sputnik 2*. Good dog!

2014 One World Trade Center, also known as the Freedom Tower, officially opens, rising as a symbol of hope and strength on the grounds where terrorist attacks destroyed the Twin Towers on September 11, 2001.

NOVEMBER 4

1863 — Benjamin Franklin Palmer patents the artificial leg, replacing wooden peg legs with a design that uses springs and metal tendons that mimic the movement of joints. This innovation gave people much more comfort and flexibility when they moved around.

1879 — **Dayton, Ohio, saloon owner James Ritty, with the help of his mechanic brother, invents the cash register**, mostly because his employees were stealing from him and he needed a way to track sales. When filing the patent, he calls it "Ritty's Incorruptible Cashier."

1939 — Hey man, cool car! Automobile maker Packard offers the first air-conditioned car to the sweaty public.

NOVEMBER 5

★ It's National Doughnut Day!

These deep-fried delicacies rolled into our lives in the 1800s thanks to Elizabeth Gregory, the mother of ship captain Hanson Gregory. She made the doughy delights using spices like cinnamon and nutmeg, believing they would help Hanson and his crewmates fight off scurvy and colds on long voyages. She put hazelnuts or walnuts in the center and called the dough with nuts doughnuts. Years later, Captain Hanson claimed credit for putting a hole in the middle. Did he do that to save money on ingredients or because they're more fun to eat that way? We'll guess both!

1605 — The Gunpowder Plot, a conspiracy of English Roman Catholics to blow up Parliament, King James I, and his family, is foiled. This day is now known in England as Guy Fawkes Day, named after one of the plot's main conspirators. The failed explosion is ironically celebrated with fireworks and bonfires where effigies (simplistic models almost like scarecrows) of Guy Fawkes are burned.

1998 — Scientists announce they are able to isolate a primitive kind of cell in our bone marrow—called stem cells—that can be used to grow bones, heart muscle, nerves, organs, and tissue for people with various diseases.

NOVEMBER 6

Who wants a chip loaded with cheesy-gooey historical goodness? Nachos were invented in 1940 at the Victory Club in Piedras, Mexico. Legend has it that a group of tourists came in after hours looking for something to eat. The kitchen was closed, so the maître d', Ignacio Anaya, went into the kitchen and made a quick dish with ingredients he found: tortilla chips, cheese, and slices of pickled jalapeños. The tourists loved it so much, they referred to it afterward by Ignacio's nickname which was Nacho. The dish gained popularity and soon other restaurants were making it. Anaya eventually moved to Eagle Pass, Texas where he opened his own restaurant called, naturally, Nacho's.

1869 ● Once upon a time, Saturdays in fall were not devoted to college football. But when the whistle blew on this day, **Rutgers and New Jersey (Princeton) went head-to-head.** They didn't go helmet-to-helmet because there were no helmets back then. In fact, the game was almost a totally different sport from what we know today. Back then, football teams tried to kick the ball into the opponent's goal, and although they were allowed to move the ball by punching it, carrying or throwing it was against the rules. Oh, and in case you were wondering, Rutgers won that first game 6-4.

NEW!

1905 ● Spanish engineer Leonardo Torres-Quevedo makes a public demonstration of his device, the first remote controller he calls the Telekino. He uses it to operate a boat that is more than a mile away. Can you imagine if remote controls were never invented? Where would we find tiny enough pilots to fly our drones?

1989 ● Per Apple Music, rapper Queen Latifah releases her debut album, *All Hail the Queen*, on this day, redefining the previously male-dominated rap genre. Latifah influeces great female artists to come and earns a spot on the Hollywood Walk of Fame.

2000 ● The presidential election results between George W. Bush and Al Gore are officially declared "too close to call." It took a month of recounts, examining defective ballots to try to guess who the voter was trying to vote for, and arguing before the Supreme Court to determine the winner. Bush eventually won and became the fourth president to lose to the popular vote but win via electoral votes. In 2016, President Trump became the fifth president to do so.

What Are Electoral Votes?

The president and vice president of the United States aren't elected because the most people voted for them (the popular vote). The Constitution set it up as an indirect election, where the votes come from state-appointed electors. Together, they are known as the electoral college. There are 538 total electoral votes, and to win, a presidential candidate must get at least 270 electoral votes. The number of electoral votes each state has depends on its size. In 48 states and Washington, D.C., whoever wins the most popular votes receives all of a state's electoral votes. Maine and Nebraska have a system that uses proportions, where votes are given based on district and statewide results. If that sounds confusing, that's because it is. Why do we have such a complicated system? It was a compromise during the Constitutional Convention. Some feared that Congress might get involved in deciding who would become president, which could lead to corruption, and others worried that if the American people directly elected the president, they might pick someone who was unfit for the job.

2020 ● Chris Nikic becomes the first person with Down syndrome to complete an Ironman triathlon. The 21-year-old Floridian swam 2.4 miles in the Gulf of Mexico, biked 112 miles through Panama City Beach, and then ran a full 26.2-mile marathon. He finished in 16 hours 46 minutes and 9 seconds. Go, Chris, go!

NOVEMBER 8

1847 • Watch your neck. Today is the birthday of writer Bram Stoker, who wrote the original *Dracula* novel.

1892 • Grover Cleveland becomes the only president in U.S. history to win a nonconsecutive second term. He was the 22nd and 24th president. (He took an unwanted vacation from the White House when Benjamin Harrison beat him to become the 23rd prez in 1888.)

1895 • Physicist Wilhelm Conrad Röntgen discovers X-rays, which will revolutionize medical treatments by allowing doctors to take pictures of the bones hidden behind skin and muscle. He was awarded the first Nobel Prize for physics. Not bad for a guy who was once kicked out of school after getting blamed for pranking another student. (True story!)

Was Dracula a Real Person?

Don't panic, but the answer is yes. Kind of. The writer Bram Stoker based the fictional character Dracula on folktales about scary "undead" creatures and on a real person named Vlad the Impaler. Vlad was born in Transylvania, and as the son of nobleman Vlad II Dracul, he took the name Dracula. He became the ruler of Wallachia (now part of Romania), and let's just say he wasn't a nice guy. He was known for extreme brutality against his enemies, like driving wooden stakes through their bodies and leaving them to die in the cold. Some reports say that he liked to dip his bread in their blood for a snack. As we said, not a nice guy. But at least he didn't turn into a bat. That's something, right?

NOVEMBER 9

1962 • Comedy legend Lucille Ball, whom you might know from *I Love Lucy* repeats, wasn't just hilarious—she was a kick-butt boss. **On this day, Ball took over for her ex-husband Desi Arnaz as the president of Desilu Productions, becoming the first woman to control a major production studio.** Desilu produced TV shows like *Star Trek* and *Mission Impossible*, which later became iconic franchises on the small and big screens.

2015 • San Diego's SeaWorld announces it will change its killer whale show (which featured whales doing jumps and other tricks) after the documentary *Blackfish* highlighted the mistreatment of the animals. A year later, SeaWorld announced it would no longer breed killer whales and that those in their care will be the last generation to live at the park.

NOVEMBER 10

? Did You Know?

When the Revolutionary War ended, the U.S. sold the Navy's ships and disbanded the Continental Navy and the Marines. They soon realized that this was a bad idea and reestablished the forces a few years later.

COME BACK!

1775 — The Continental Congress authorizes the formation of the Marine Corps, an elite group of fighters who serve on both land and sea.

1903 — After sitting in a streetcar in New York City that had to pull over because the driver couldn't see through the sleet-covered windshield, Mary Anderson had a brilliant idea: What if something could wipe it clear while the car was moving? On this day, her idea is patented—the windshield wiper.

1969 — *Sesame Street* premieres, teaching kids how to count, spell, and share...sometimes. In the words of Cookie Monster, "I'd give you a cookie, but I ate it."

NOVEMBER 11

1918 — After more than four bloody years of fighting that resulted in the death of millions, an armistice (a truce) is signed, bringing World War I to an end.

1926 — **The American Association of State Highway Officials formally adopts the 2,448-mile path from Chicago to Los Angeles called Route 66.** Known as the Main Street of America, it served as the primary road for Americans migrating West in the early and mid-1900s.

? Did You Know?

There were several armistices that ended fighting on several fronts of World War I, but the one recognized as the end of the war was the one signed on the 11th hour of the 11th day of the 11th month.

1947 — It's Veterans Day! The first Veterans Day parade is held in Birmingham, Alabama. For a long time, this day was known as Armistice Day, celebrating the end of World War I. But in 1954, President Eisenhower signed a bill that officially proclaimed November 11 as Veterans Day, honoring all American veterans of all wars.

NOVEMBER 12

1859 • "He flies through the air with the greatest of ease, the daring young man on the flying trapeze": So went the lyrics of a song about **Jules Léotard, a French acrobat who performed the first flying-trapeze act.** Bonus invention? The leotards that dancers wear today are named after him because of the outfit he wore while flipping and swinging.

1966 • **Buzz Aldrin might have been the second human to step on the moon, but he is the first to take a space selfie.** The photo was taken a few years before the moon mission while he was aboard the *Gemini 10*. First selfie or first step, which do you think had a bigger impact on human history?

1993 • The first Ultimate Fighting Championship takes place at the McNichols Sports Arena in Denver. About 7,800 people watched in person, while another 83,000 watched on Pay-Per-View. In terms of popularity, you could say the UFC was a knockout. In 2018, UFC's lightweight championship bout between Khabib Nurmagomedov and Conor McGregor had 2.4 million PPV viewers.

NOVEMBER 13

1946 Let it snow! Scientist Vincent Schaefer seeds the clouds over Mount Greylock, Massachusetts, with pellets of dry ice and creates the first artificial snow.

1982 **The Vietnam Veterans Memorial is dedicated in Washington, D.C.** Designed by 21-year-old artist Maya Lin, the monument's black-granite wall was inscribed with the names of 57,939 Americans who died in the war. An additional 379 names have been added in subsequent years. Rather than a more typical heroic statue, Lin said she wanted the memorial's V-shape to evoke a "wound that is closed and healing."

2020 Kim Ng takes over as general manager of the Miami Marlins, making her the first female GM in Major League Baseball history—and the first woman to hold that title in any major North American men's sports leagues!

NOVEMBER 14

1902 While on an unsuccessful hunting trip, **President Theodore Roosevelt refuses to shoot a bear that is tied up to a tree.** His act of compassion results in a national toy craze known as the teddy bear.

1960 **Six-year-old and very brave Ruby Bridges becomes the first Black student to integrate an elementary school in the South.** She broke the color line by attending the all-white William Frantz Elementary School, which is a few blocks from her family's home in New Orleans. A statue of Ruby now stands on the grounds of her old school, which is now called the Akili Academy.

NOVEMBER 15

1887 • Artist Georgia O'Keeffe is born. Considered the mother of American modernism, she painted the beautiful and powerful abstract forms she saw in nature.

1969 • **Dave Thomas opens the first Wendy's in Columbus, Ohio.** So, who is Wendy? His daughter...whose name is Melinda. Wait, what? Melinda's nickname was Wendy, because her siblings couldn't pronounce her name and started calling her Wenda, which eventually turned into Wendy.

2001 • The Xbox gaming console is released, going head-to-head with Sony's PlayStation 2 and Nintendo's GameCube. Its makers named it Xbox because of the DirectX technology inside that allows gaming software to work with video screens, speakers, and headphones. (Pretty dorky explanation for something that sounds so cool.)

2017 • Leonardo da Vinci's painting *Salvator Mundi* sells for $450.3 million at auction in New York City, setting a world record price tag for artwork. That's $10,000 per brushstroke!

NOVEMBER 16

1974 • **Astronomers beam a very, very, very long-distance message to the M13 star cluster,** which is 25,000 light-years away. Known as the Arecibo Message, it contains information about our planet, our DNA, and our chemical makeup, all in a primary-number system code. Let's hope any aliens it reaches are good at math!

★ **It's National Fast-Food Day!**

You likely know that Ronald McDonald isn't a real person, but did you know that KFC's Colonel Sanders actually was a colonel? Well, sort of KFC founder Harland David Sanders was never in the military, but in 1939, Kentucky Governor Rudy Laffoon made him official by naming him as an honorary colonel.

NOVEMBER 17

1869
The Suez Canal opens, connecting the Mediterranean Sea and the Red Sea. While it started relatively small, it has expanded, and now every year, about 19,000 ships carrying $1 trillion worth of goods pass through it.

1996
Dwayne "the Rock" Johnson makes his professional wrestling debut. Despite sporting what he later described as an "awful haircut" during his first match, he became a massive star in the ring—and eventually also one of the most successful movie stars of all time.

2003
In other muscle-y news, on this day action movie superstar Arnold Schwarzenegger is sworn in as governor of California. Born in Austria, Arnold became a U.S. citizen in 1983. After serving two terms as governor, he returned to moviemaking. Will we ever see Mr. Muscles in the White House? Sorry, Arnie, but no chance. The Constitution states that a candidate must be born in America or be a natural-born citizen (for example, a child born to American parents serving in the military overseas) to be eligible.

NOVEMBER 18

2011
The first full version of Minecraft is released. Every day, millions of players jump into this infinite digital sandbox to build, dig, and on occasion, fight off creepers and other weird monsters roaming around.

The game's signature monsters, Creepers, were an accident. Designer Markus Persson was trying to make a pig but messed up the coding, which resulted in the bizarre-looking and beloved beings.

CLOSE ENOUGH.

1805

The Lewis and Clark Expedition finally reaches the Pacific Ocean after setting out from St. Louis on May 14, 1804. Led by Captain Meriwether Lewis and Lieutenant William Clark, the Corps of Discovery team's mission, set by President Thomas Jefferson, was to explore the Missouri River, form contacts with Native Americans, and find an all-water route to the Pacific Ocean. The route didn't exist, but with the help of many Native Americans, in particular a 16-year-old Shoshone woman named Sacagawea, the two men were able to map uncharted land, rivers, and mountains, and inspire others to explore the American West.

❓ Did You Know?

Four score and seven years ago is a fancy way of saying "87 years ago." A score is 20 years.

1863

President Abraham Lincoln delivers the Gettysburg Address, one of the most famous speeches in American history. It was made at the National Cemetery of Gettysburg where a horribly bloody Civil War battle was fought and won by the Union. It began, "Four score and seven years ago our fathers brought forth, upon this continent, a new nation, conceived in liberty, and dedicated to the proposition that all men are created equal." Lincoln believed that the Civil War was a test to see if the nation would survive or "perish from the earth."

1895

Lincoln might have had an easier time writing and editing the Gettysburg Address if he had a pencil, which wasn't patented until this day by American inventor Frederick E. Blaisdell.

NOVEMBER 20

1851

American whaling ship *Essex* is rammed by a sperm whale and sinks. Whales 1, people 0. This incident inspired writer Herman Melville's book *Moby Dick*, which is regarded as one of the greatest novels ever written. (Today, at least. When it was released, the book bombed.)

1866

Cincinnati inventors James L. Haven and Charles Hettrick patent a toy called the Whirligig, better known as the yo-yo.

How Does a Yo-Yo Work?

When you flick your wound-up yo-yo, gravity pulls it down, creating kinetic energy (the energy of motion). It unwinds and rotates as it drops until it hits the end of the string, where it continues to spin on the loose loop tied around the yo-yo's axle. When you flick your finger up, it creates friction and the axle grabs the string again, allowing the yo-yo to zip back up to your hand.

1964 • Stretching from Staten Island to Brooklyn, **the Verrazano Narrows Bridge opens** to traffic, beating the Golden Gate Bridge as the longest suspension bridge in the world at the time. Its tower-to-tower central span is 4,260 feet, but if you've ever been stuck in traffic on it, it feels like that span is more like 4,260 miles.

❷ Did You Know?

The current title holder of the longest suspension bridge in the world is the 1915 Çanakkale Bridge in Turkey, with a span that is 2,000 feet longer than the Verrazano. Construction began in 2017, but it is called the 1915 bridge to commemorate an important naval victory for the country during World War I.

1976 • The movie *Rocky*, written by and starring Sylvester Stallone, premieres. About an underdog boxer, the movie became immensely popular and was followed by multiple sequels and the *Creed* series spin-off— a $1.7 billion franchise and growing.

❷ Did You Know?

Sylvester Stallone was so broke before making *Rocky*, he had to sell his dog Butkus for $40 in order to buy himself food. After he sold the screenplay, Stallone was able to buy his dog back—and the guy charged him $15,000! But Stallone said, "He was worth every penny!"

NOVEMBER 22

1963 President John F. Kennedy is assassinated by Lee Harvey Oswald while riding in an open-topped car through Dallas. As Kennedy's car passed in front of the Texas School Book Depository Building, Oswald fired three shots from the sixth floor, killing Kennedy and seriously injuring Texas Governor John Connally. Two days later, while being transferred by police to another jail, Oswald was killed by a man named Jack Ruby. Ruby had connections to the Mafia, which made some speculate that he killed Oswald to silence him and cover up a bigger conspiracy. Those accusations were never proven, and Ruby swore to his dying day that he shot Oswald out of grief for the president.

1995 To infinity and beyond! **Toy Story, the first fully computer-generated animated feature film, is released.**

❓ Did You Know?

In the Pixar movie *Cars*, Lightning McQueen's number is 95—a reference to the fact that Pixar's first flick, *Toy Story*, was made in 1995. Also, all the *Cars* characters ride on Lightyear Tires which is an homage to *Toy Story*'s Buzz Lightyear.

NOVEMBER 23

1889 The world's first jukebox is installed at the Palais Royale Saloon in San Francisco. Since speakers were not invented yet, customers listened to the music by holding long tubes up to their ears, kind of like early headphones. Must have made it hard to dance!

1936 **Legendary blues musician Robert Johnson has his first recording session at the Gunter Hotel in San Antonio.** Those recordings would go on to influence the biggest names in rock and roll. Johnson was so good at guitar, there was a legend that he sold his soul to the devil in exchange for musical talent.

1971 • **A man calling himself Dan Cooper boards a plane in Oregon heading to Seattle.** Once in the air, he tells a flight attendant that he will blow up the plane with a bomb hidden in his suitcase unless he is given $200,000 and four parachutes. After landing in Seattle, Cooper is given his demands, the passengers get off, and Cooper commands the pilot to fly him to Mexico City. Then, somewhere between Seattle and Reno, Nevada, Cooper jumps out of the plane with a parachute and the money. He was never found, and his disappearance and true identity remain a mystery. Over the years, he has been referred to as D.B. Cooper, but the FBI say that was a name invented by the press.

1974 • **Anthropology professor Donald Johanson and his research assistant Tom Gray discover fossils of an early human ancestor in Ethiopia.** Nicknamed Lucy, the remains revealed that humans walked upright more than 3 million years ago. Why the name Lucy? The scientists listened to the Beatles' song "Lucy in the Sky with Diamonds" while they celebrated their discovery that night.

NOVEMBER 25

1948

After seeing this new thing called a TV demonstrated at a convention, Oregon radio station owner Leroy "Ed" Parsons and his wife really wanted one in their home. Trouble was, at that time there were very few TV stations on the West Coast. So you could own a TV set but there was no way to watch anything on it. That is until he figured out how to capture a weak TV signal that originated in Seattle from the rooftop of a hotel across the street from him and was able to transfer that signal to their apartment. **Once word got out that the Parsons had TV, their home became a tourist destination.** "People would drive for hundreds of miles to see television," he explained. Determined to get these people of out his home, he used wires to connect the signal to other TV sets. And so, that's how Parsons became the inventor of cable TV.

NOVEMBER 26

1917

The National Hockey League is founded with five Canadian teams: the Montreal Canadiens, Montreal Wanderers, Ottawa Senators, Toronto Arenas, and Quebec Bulldogs. The first American team, the Boston Bruins, was added in 1924. If you think hockey is a tough sport now, back then, goalies didn't even have face masks. Between all six teams, we'll guess there were about six teeth left in the players' mouths.

1920 • **The silent movie *The Mark of Zorro* starring Douglas Fairbanks is released.** It follows the adventures of a masked swordsman who protects peasants from rich and powerful bad guys. Many people say it is the first superhero film.

1924 • The Macy's Thanksgiving Day Parade marches for the first time, starting in Harlem and going six miles down to 34th Street in New York City. Like today, there were costumed employees, floats, and Santa Claus, but no giant balloon animals. Instead, they had real animals! An assortment of bears, monkeys, elephants, and camels on loan from the Central Park Zoo marched in the parade. (Apparently, they couldn't get a cab.)

Who Was Bruce Lee?

Bruce Lee was a famous actor and martial arts expert whose amazing skills inspired many of the coolest fight scenes we see today in movies like *The Matrix*. Lee was born in 1940 in San Francisco and grew up in Hong Kong, where he appeared in more than 20 movies as a child performer. At the age of 18, he moved to America and, while putting on a martial arts demonstration, was discovered by Hollywood. He costarred in the TV show *The Green Hornet* and made the super famous fight flick *Enter the Dragon*. Lee sadly died before the movie was released, but the film knocked everyone out and influenced future action stars ranging from Jackie Chan to Brad Pitt. Lee was such an expert that he even invented his own style of fighting called Jeet Kune Do which translates to "the way of the intercepting fist." Sounds painful!

1940 • **Martial arts great Bruce Lee is born in San Francisco, California.** He does not get into an epic brawl in the hospital nursery (we think?...).

2013 • *Frozen* is released in the United States and becomes one of the highest-grossing animated movies of all time. It technically took 76 years to get made. Walt Disney said that he wanted to adapt the original story, "The Snow Queen," by Hans Christian Andersen, way back in 1937. Guess he couldn't let the idea go—*let it gooooo.*

NOVEMBER 28

1720 — **Two of the few female pirates to terrorize the high seas, Mary Read and Anne Bonny, go on trial in Jamaica for crimes including stealing a vessel in the Bahamas.** They were convicted and sentenced to death. Their executions were postponed because both were pregnant, and Bonny was eventually freed, while Read (who pretended to be a man during a lot of her time as a pirate) died in prison.

NOVEMBER 29

1972 — **Atari announces the release of video game Pong.** The game involved players moving paddles up and down to stop a ball from going into their goal. It was incredibly simple, the graphics incredibly basic, and it was *incredibly* popular. Pong was the first commercially successful video game, creating an industry that accounts for nearly $100 billion in sales every year.

1972 — President Gerald Ford signs the Education for All Handicapped Children Act, which guarantees education and support for children with disabilities and their families.

1954 ● **Ann Hodges, a 34-year-old woman, was napping in her home in Alabama when a nine-pound meteorite crashed through the ceiling.** It bounced off a radio and banged into her thigh, making her the first and only person to be inured by a meteorite. Lucky?

2017 ● **Students and staff of Chinese Culture University record the longest-lasting rainbow ever.** It stretches across the sky for a total of 8 hours and 58 minutes. It earned a Guinness World Record (hooray!), but sadly there was no pot of gold at the end of it (boo!).

THIS DAY IN *my* HISTORY
NOVEMBER

Fill in any memorable events from your life here.

1 ....

2 ....

3 ....

4 ....

5 ....

6 ....

7 ....

8 ....

9 ....

10 ....

11 ....

12 ....

13 ....

14 ....

15 ....

16 ....

17 ....

18 ....

19 ....

20 ....

21 ....

22 ....

23 ....

24 ....

25 ....

26 ....

27 ....

28 ....

29 ....

30 ....

DECEMBER 1

1761
Happy birthday to Madame Tussaud, a famous wax sculpture artist of hyperrealistic statues of celebrities, politicians, and real-life bad guys. Her works were super popular back then and still are today, with 21 Madame Tussauds museums scattered around the world. Tussaud's talent for making eerily perfect sculptures has a pretty eerie origin story. She claimed to have perfected her craft during the Reign of Terror, a bloody period of the French Revolution, when, she said, she was responsible for making death masks from heads chopped off by the guillotine.

1887
World-famous detective character Sherlock Holmes makes his first appearance in the novel *Study in Scarlet* by Arthur Conan Doyle. Mysteriously, neither the story nor the detective got much notice. But then in 1891, Doyle began publishing Sherlock Holmes short stories in the *Strand Magazine*, and the case-cracking character became a worldwide sensation. Mystery solved!

1955
In Montgomery, Alabama, an NAACP field secretary and seamstress named Rosa Parks is arrested and put in jail for refusing to give up her seat on a public bus to a white man. Her arrest sparked the Montgomery Bus Boycott, which was organized by a young Martin Luther King, Jr., and involved tens of thousands of people refusing to ride on the buses for more than an entire year. On November 13, 1956, the U.S. Supreme Court ruled that the city bus segregation laws were a violation of the 14th Amendment. Parks is known as the mother of the civil rights movement, and following her death in 2005, Congress honored Parks by making her the first woman to lie in state in the Capitol Rotunda.

DECEMBER 2

1823 — President James Monroe sets forth the Monroe Doctrine, which warns European nations not to attempt further colonization or military intervention in the Western Hemisphere, or else the United States will see those actions as threats. Basically, it said that the Western Hemisphere was America's, so back off! It proved to be a controversial decision, but the Monroe Doctrine influenced American diplomacy for more than a century.

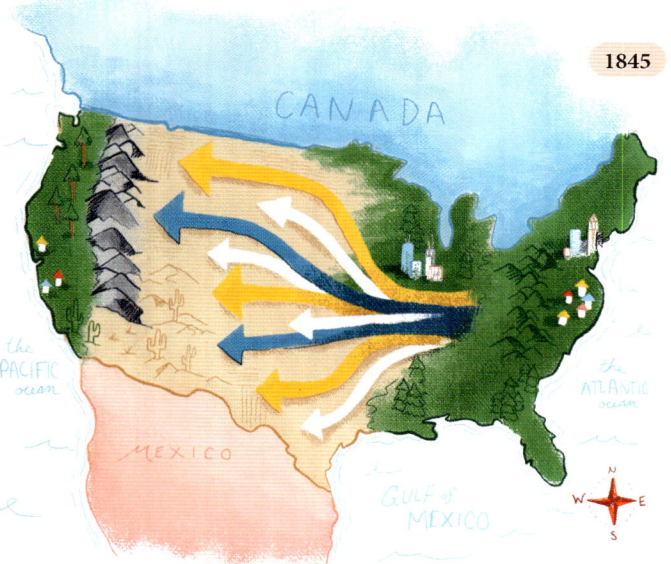

1845 — An important day for presidents declaring stuff! **In President James K. Polk's first State of the Union address, he declares that the United States should expand westward.** The concept became known as *manifest destiny*, a term coined by newspaper editor John O'Sullivan. Manifest destiny was the belief (considered controversial by many historians for its destructive impact on America's native populations) that the United States was destined by God to expand its borders, spreading democracy and capitalism across the entire continent of North America.

1982 — Dr. Barney Clark becomes the recipient of the world's first permanent artificial heart. Called the Jarvik-7 (named after inventor Robert Jarvik, MD), the aluminum and polyurethane device was successful—and more than a little bit cumbersome. To keep working, it had to be connected to a 400-pound air compressor.

2017 — Is pepperoni less filling if it is weightless? **Astronauts on the International Space Station receive a very welcome package in a resupply shipment—all of the ingredients to make pizza!** It is the first time pizza is made in space, much to the delight of all onboard the ISS. NASA astronaut Randy Bresnik happily tweeted, "Flying Saucers of the edible kind."

1689 • Swiss surgeon Johannes Fatio completes the first recorded successful separation of conjoined newborn twin girls. Elisabeth and Catherina were born joined near the sternum and the navel. Once separated, they recovered fully from the surgery and lived normal lives.

What Was the Cold War?

The Cold War was a fierce rivalry between the United States and the Soviet Union that began after World War II and lasted decades. The two superpowers mistrusted one another and didn't want the other to gain too much global strength, which led to massive buildups of conventional and nuclear weapons. The U.S. and Soviet Union also got involved in conflicts like the Korean War, the Congo Civil War, and the Vietnam War, where each superpower supported the opposite side.

1832 • Jonathan the tortoise is born. Who is Jonathan? He's a tortoise believed to be the oldest animal on land. Because Jonathan is close to 200 years old and still crawling around—very, *very* slowly—the world celebrates his birthday on this day.

1989 • At the first-ever summit held between the two leaders, Soviet President Mikhail Gorbachev and U.S. president George H. W. Bush suggest that the Cold War could finally be coming to an end.

1992 • **Software programmer Neil Papworth sends the first-ever text message from a computer to his colleague.** It reads simply, "Merry Christmas." (Hey, we said he was a great programmer, not a great novelist.)

DECEMBER 4

1875 • New York City's William M. "Boss" Tweed escapes from jail after being arrested for stealing tens of millions of the city's dollars. While in hiding, Tweed was put on trial in absentia (meaning while he was not present) and found guilty. He escaped to Spain, where he lived as a seaman for a year. But when someone recognized him from a political cartoon about his escape, he was captured and returned to New York City to serve out his sentence. Boss Tweed, you're fired!

2012 • Paleontologist Sterling Nesbitt and his colleagues publish their study of *Nyasasaurus parringtoni fossils*, the oldest known dinosaur that lived about 245 million years ago. It's old but not big. Nesbitt describes it as a long-legged, long-necked creature that was "the size of a Labrador retriever." Can you teach an old dinosaur new tricks?

DECEMBER 5

1872 — **Creepy cruise: British sailors in the Atlantic spot a ship bouncing around in the waves. After investigating, they learn it is the *Mary Celeste*, which had left New York City eight days before.** Once onboard, they found all of the ship's supplies and cargo, but no sign of its 10 crew members. Theories ranging from sea monsters to a pirate attack to the crew abandoning ship have all been floated, but no one has been able to definitively prove what became of the men of the *Mary Celeste*.

1945 — In other weird news, five U.S. Navy Avenger torpedo bombers take off for a training run from the Ft. Lauderdale Naval Air Station in Florida and never return. Hundreds of ships and aircraft searched thousands of square miles of their flight path, an area known as the Bermuda Triangle, but no trace of the crew members or aircraft of the Lost Squadron was ever found.

What Is the Bermuda Triangle?

The Bermuda Triangle is an area of the Atlantic Ocean between Miami, Bermuda, and Puerto Rico. Dozens of ships and airplanes have disappeared in this triangle without a trace. Sometimes, as with the Lost Squadron, pilots report by radio that they've become disoriented before disappearing. Other times, boats and planes have gone missing in good weather without ever radioing for help. Freaky!

DECEMBER 6

1884 • A nine-inch aluminum pyramid inscribed with the words *Laus Deo*, (Latin for "praise be to God") is placed on top of the Washington Monument, literally capping off the 36-year construction project. The 555-foot structure is made up of an incredible 36,000 blocks of marble and granite. Think of it as the world's largest Jenga.

1999 • As a social-justice fighter for the rights of workers, immigrants, women, and young people, **Dolores Huerta receives the Eleanor Roosevelt Award for Human Rights.** She received many awards for her tireless efforts, including the Presidential Medal of Freedom in 2012.

2017 • **Scientists announce the discovery of the oldest black hole in the universe.** Formed approximately 690 million years after the big bang, it is not only billions of years old, it is huge. How huge? About 800 million times bigger than the sun.

What Is a Black Hole?

It's a place in space where gravity is so strong that not even light can escape its pull. Black holes are typically formed when an aging star collapses. But don't worry, our sun is way too puny to form a black hole, so earth will never be swallowed by one of these gravity monsters. Phew!

LATELY IT FEELS LIKE HE'S ACTUALLY PUSHING US AWAY!

DECEMBER 7

1941

In the early morning hours, a squadron of Japanese warplanes dives out of the sky, launching a surprise attack on the United States Naval Base at Pearl Harbor in Hawaii. Over the course of two hours, more than 350 Japanese planes dropped bombs and kamikaze pilots purposely crashed their planes into targets, destroying and damaging 21 ships, more than 300 planes, and killing more than 2,300 Americans. The next day, President Franklin Roosevelt proclaimed December 7, 1941, as "a date which will live in infamy." Congress declared war on Japan, and so two years after it began, the United States entered World War II.

Why Did Japan Attack Pearl Harbor?

The sneak attack was planned by Admiral Isoroku Yamamoto, who was once a student at Harvard University. Given all of America's resources, Yamamoto was sure that Japan could not win a long, drawn-out war with the United States. He believed that Japan's only chance for victory was a surprise attack that would take the U.S. naval fleet out of action for at least a year. But despite the destruction caused in that shocking ambush, Yamamoto's goal of crippling the navy failed. There were no U.S. aircraft carriers at Pearl Harbor that day and the navy's repair shops and fueling stations were mostly left unharmed.

2013 • With a show put on at the Carlini Argentine Base in Antarctica, heavy-metal rockers Metallica becomes the first band to play on all seven continents in a single year. The show was performed for contest winners from Latin America, research scientists stationed in Antarctica, and the crew of the ship that brought the group over. Are penguins big metalheads now? We'll never know. To protect the environment from noise pollution, Metallica's music was transmitted to special headphones for audience members.

DECEMBER 9

What Is the Heisman Trophy?

The Heisman Trophy is given out every year to the most outstanding player in college football, as voted by a poll of sportswriters. In the second year of its existence, the name was changed from the DAC Trophy to the Heisman to honor legendary college football coach John William Heisman, who transformed many rules of the game, including adding the forward pass.

1935 • **The Downtown Athletic Club presents the first Heisman award—originally called the DAC Trophy—to Jay Berwanger, a player for the University of Chicago football team.** Berwanger called plays, ran the ball, threw passes, punted, tackled, kicked off, kicked extra points, and returned punts, earning him the much-deserved nickname the One-Man Team.

1959 • At the DeMille Theatre in New York City, a showing of the travelog movie *Behind the Great Wall* is enhanced by pumping aromas into the theater that match what viewers are seeing: food, smoke, incense, and the like. One reviewer for the *New York Times* was less than happy with his nose's experience, writing, "When this viewer emerged from the theater, he happily filled his lungs with that lovely fume-laden New York ozone. It never has smelled so good." Guess it isn't a surprise that smell-o-vision never caught on.

DECEMBER 10

1911 • **Marie Curie wins her second Nobel Prize for her work in radioactivity, discovering the elements radium and polonium.** During World War I, she oversaw the creation of mobile radiology units that were used to help doctors treat more than a million wounded soldiers. After she died, Curie's notebooks were placed in lead-lined boxes in France as they were contaminated with dangerous radium and will remain radioactive for more than 1,000 years.

2020 • A Little Free Library built by atmospheric scientist Dr. Russell Schnell is set up on the South Pole, officially putting little libraries on every continent. Who wants a frozen bookcicle?

DECEMBER 11

1913 • **King Edward VIII becomes the first English monarch to voluntarily abdicate the throne.** He chose to do so after the Church of England, British leaders and the public criticized his decision to marry Wallis Warfield Simpson, an American divorcée.

1946 • United Nations International Children's Emergency Fund (UNICEF) launches, devoted to improving the lives of children with better nutrition, education, and medical care.

DECEMBER 12

1925

In the town of San Luis Obispo, which is about halfway between Los Angeles and San Francisco, **the Milestone Mo-Tel Inn opens.** The world's first motel (short for motor hotel) was pretty snazzy compared to the dives we think about today, and it cost travelers only $1.25 per night—super cheap even back then. Before the Mo-Tel opened, tired travelers had to pull their cars into empty lots or gas stations and snooze in the back seat.

2015

In France, 196 countries come together for the Paris Agreement. The agreement is a legal treaty designed to slow and reverse climate change by cutting greenhouse gas emissions and adopting other sustainability measures.

DECEMBER 13

1972

"Goodnight moon." **Apollo 17's mission ends, the sixth and last time humans stepped foot on the lunar surface.** NASA has recently announced the Artemis program, which intends to not only send humans back to the moon but also set up a long-term moon base while they're up there. Next stop for humans? Mars.

2013

Snow falls in Cairo, Egypt. That might not seem so exciting, but it was the first time it happened in 112 years. How do you think the Sphinx did in its first snowball fight?

DECEMBER 14

1911 • **Norwegian explorer Roald Amundsen becomes the first explorer to reach the South Pole**, beating his British rival, Robert Falcon Scott—who was racing to the same icy spot—by more than a month. Eat my frozen dust!

1947 • Stock car driver and race promoter William H.G. France holds a meeting in Daytona Beach, Florida, with a few dozen drivers, car owners, promoters, mechanics, and journalists. The result? The formation of the National Association for Stock Car Auto Racing, better known as NASCAR. (We'll guess it was a very, very fast meeting.)

2020 • Northwell Health critical care nurse Sandra Lindsay becomes the first person in the United States to get the COVID-19 vaccine.

2021 • Steph Curry makes his 2,974th three-point shot, breaking Ray Allen's record for the most made three-pointers in NBA history. The son of NBA great Dell Curry, Steph basically grew up on basketball courts. The only thing his dad didn't teach him was how to miss!

DECEMBER 15

1791 • **The Bill of Rights is officially adopted, becoming amendments 1 through 10 to the Constitution.** These amendments protect Americans' civil liberties such as the freedom of speech, press, and religion.

2015 • The world's largest suspended piñata—61 feet tall, 60 feet long, and 23 feet wide—is hung up at Plaza de Los Mártires in Mexico. It is filled with thousands of balls, hundreds of Barbie dolls, and nearly 700 pounds of candy and chocolate. If the piñata was that huge, how big was the stick they used to whack it?

1707 Mount Fuji kicks some ash. This day is the last time Mount Fuji, Japan's highest point, erupted. Fuji is actually made of many overlapping volcanoes. The top two are named Old Fuji and Young Fuji. When Mount Fuji erupted, it spit up tons of tephra, which is made up of solid material like ash and rock, unlike lava, which is molten. Mount Fuji is still an active volcano, so this was the last time it erupted, but likely it won't be its last.

1773 Anyone care for a cup of tea? **A group of American colonists known as the Sons of Liberty dump 342 chests of tea imported by the British East India Company into Boston Harbor.** No, they weren't trying to give the fish an afternoon caffeine fix—they did it to protest British taxes on the colonies.

2020 Billionaire MacKenzie Scott, an author who was once married to Amazon founder Jeff Bezos, announced that she donated nearly $4.2 billion to organizations focused on aiding those in need, including Meals on Wheels, Goodwill, and multiple college scholarship programs.

DECEMBER 17

1903 **Orville and Wilbur Wright make the first sustained manned, heavier-than-air aircraft flight at Kitty Hawk, North Carolina.** Piloted by Wilbur, their plane flew for 59 seconds and traveled 852 feet. The brother's feat was disbelieved by many in the U.S., so they went overseas to Europe where they performed demonstrations and gave plane rides to heads of government and journalists (no mid-flight snacks, unfortunately). The brothers became wealthy businessmen from selling their flying invention, which they continued to fine-tune and evolve with new models for nearly 20 years.

How Do Airplanes Fly?

When air flows over an airplane's wings, the shape of the wing makes air flow faster over the top of it than underneath it. This results in lift. Thrust, created by a propeller or engine, is the force that pushes and pulls an airplane against gravity. (Barf bags are the things that prevent you from making a huge mess on airplanes, but we won't get into that now.)

ANY SNACKS on this FLIGHT?

DECEMBER 18

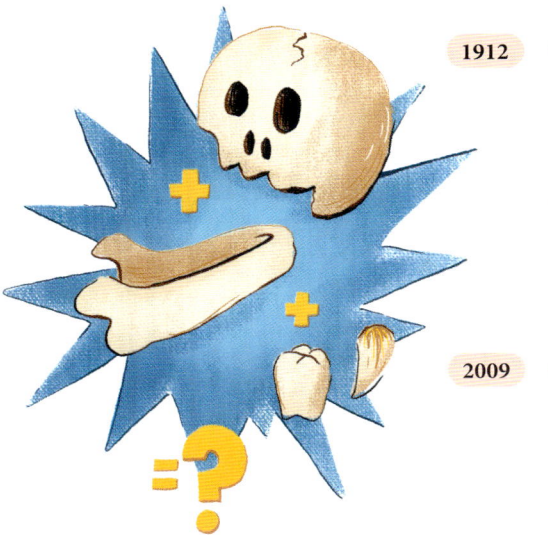

1912 • **Amateur archaeologist Charles Dawson, digging in the Piltdown gravel pit in Sussex, England, announces he's discovered bones of the missing evolutionary link between ape and man.** Called Piltdown Man, the discovery was celebrated...and doubted. In 1953, a study of the remains with modern equipment revealed that they were actually made up of a human skull, the jaw and teeth of an orangutan, and the tooth of a chimpanzee. In other words, Piltdown Man was a hoax.

2009 • *Avatar* premieres in the U.S. Its revolutionary 3D technology wows audiences, makes some of them nauseous, and racks up a whole lot of money—the most money any movie has made in history, raking in a global box office of $2.9 billion as of 2022.

DECEMBER 19

1843 • **A Christmas Carol by Charles Dickens is published,** telling the tale of cold-hearted Ebenezer Scrooge, who is visited by the spirits of Christmases Past, Present, and Yet to Come, and is transformed into a kinder man. The story has been retold and reinterpreted countless times in movies, TV shows, and theater productions, and it was originally written by Dickens as a way of persuading his fellow Londoners to give more to the poor during the holidays.

2019 • A state of emergency is declared in Australia's New South Wales as 100 bushfires rage, spreading fast because of the high winds and a record-breaking heatwave. Nearly 70,000 square miles burned, destroying wildlife, habitats, and almost 6,000 buildings and homes.

❓ Did You Know?

Ebenezer Scrooge was a real person. Mostly. According to one origins story, while walking through a Scottish cemetery, Dickens noticed the tombstone of an Ebenezer Scroggie engraved with the words "mean man." At least that's what Dickens scribbled in his notebook. It actually read, "meal man," signifying that Scroggie was a grain merchant. And unlike the fictional Scrooge, the real guy was known to be somewhat of a party animal.

1812   Jacob and Wilhelm Grimm, better known as the Brothers Grimm, publish *Kinder-und Hausmärchen* (*Children's and Household Tales*), the first volume of a collection that became known in English as *Grimm's Fairy Tales*. The collection introduced characters like Cinderella, Sleeping Beauty, Snow White, Little Red Riding Hood, Hansel and Gretel, and many more. These original tales were a bit bloodier and grosser than Disney's movie versions. For example, in "Cinderella," the wicked stepsisters cut off their own heels and toes to fit into the glass slipper! Ouch.

1951   **In Idaho, the first functioning nuclear power plant, EBR-I, goes to work.** It starts small. On day one, it generates enough power to light four light bulbs.

2015   Four amputee British military veterans get into a rowboat in the Canary Islands, and 47 days and 3,000 miles later, pull into Antigua's English Harbour. Their journey, which took an estimated 1.4 million oar strokes, put them in the record books as the first all-amputee crew to row across the Atlantic Ocean.

DECEMBER 21

1891   **Dr. James Naismith introduces the rules of a new game he invented: basketball.** While working at the International YMCA Training School (now Springfield College) in Springfield, Massachusetts, Naismith was asked by his boss to create an indoor game to allow the students to burn off energy during the freezing cold New England winters. After some trial and error, Naismith came up with workable rules and about a week later, his class played the first basketball game using a soccer ball and two peach baskets.

The Game Has Changed!

In the original 13 rules written by Naismith, one was that players could not run with the ball. They could pass or shoot only from where they caught it. And since the game used actual baskets, a shot counted only if the ball stayed inside and didn't bounce out.

2012   A calendar created by ancient Mayans ends on this exact day, causing many doomsayers to predict it would be when the world would end. If you are reading this, then obviously they were wrong.

213

DECEMBER 22

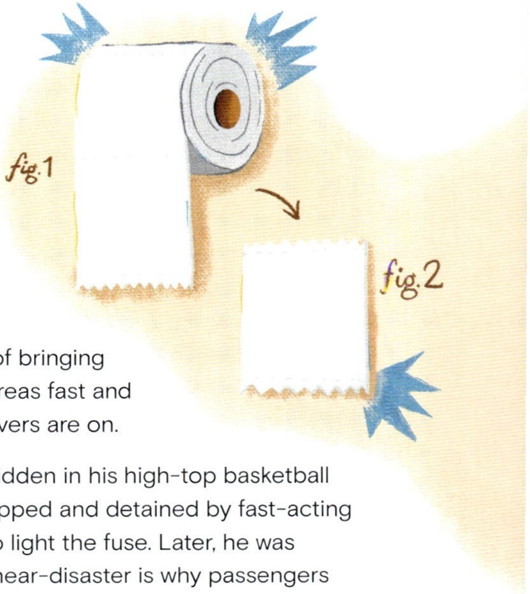

1891 — **A patent is granted to Setii Wheeler for perforated toilet paper,** making it much easier for the rest of us to tear a square when in need.

1956 — A four-pound bundle of joy—a baby gorilla named Colo—becomes the first-ever gorilla born in captivity. Think the zookeepers gave her a banana birthday cake?

1971 — Doctors Without Borders is founded, with the goal of bringing emergency medical care to war-torn and disaster areas fast and effectively, no matter which side of a conflict caregivers are on.

2001 — Terrorist Richard Reid attempts to light explosives hidden in his high-top basketball sneakers on a flight from Paris to Miami. He was stopped and detained by fast-acting crew and passengers who spotted him struggling to light the fuse. Later, he was arrested and sentenced to life without parole. This near-disaster is why passengers have to remove their shoes while going through security at airports.

2010 — President Barack Obama signs legislation to repeal the military's Don't Ask, Don't Tell policy, allowing homosexual men and women to serve in the U.S. military openly and proudly.

fig.1

fig.2

DECEMBER 23

1867 — Born to parents who were once enslaved, Sarah Breedlove (later known as Madam C.J. Walker) grows up to start her own cosmetics and hair-care company, employing thousands and becoming a self-made millionaire and philanthropist.

1888 — **Dutch painter Vincent van Gogh, known for dynamic and colorful paintings like *Starry Night,* gets into an argument with fellow artist Paul Gauguin, and in a fit of passion, chops off part of his own ear with a razor.** (This is not a good way to win an argument.)

1997 — A menorah is lit for the first time in Vatican City, the home of the Pope, signaling friendship and unity between leaders of the Jewish and Catholic faiths.

1801 • British inventor Richard Trevithick takes a bunch of pals for a ride on his "Puffing Devil," the first steam-powered passenger vehicle. The ride was fun, with one of the passengers reporting that it was, "like a little bird...going faster than I could walk." The fun was short-lived. A few days later the Puffing Devil overheated and was engulfed in flames.

1914 • **On Christmas Eve, a miracle of sorts happens during World War I.** While hunkered down in the trenches along the deadly Western Front, British machine gunner Bruce Bairnsfather heard an odd sound: the Germans singing Christmas carols. The British troops joined in, and sometime later, these men who were previously trying to kill one another climbed out of their trenches and met in the No Man's Land between their fronts. They exchanged handshakes, shared wine, sang together, and played soccer in a spontaneous party. This "Christmas Truce" was condemned by military leaders at the time, but 100 years later, it was commemorated with a statue of two hands shaking that stands in England's National Memorial Arboretum. On the day of the monument's unveiling, the English and German national soccer teams also played a friendly match, with England winning 1-0.

2008 • Supersize Santa! What was likely the world's biggest ice Santa ever is unveiled at an ice-sculpture festival in the Chinese city of Harbin. The Santa sculpture was 525 feet long, which makes us terrified to think how big his reindeer must have been.

DECEMBER 25

1776 • **General George Washington leads 5,400 troops in a daring crossing of the partially frozen Delaware River,** launching a surprise attack on enemy Hessian forces in Trenton, New Jersey. After suffering many significant defeats at the hands of the British, such as the loss of control of New York City, the success of Washington's unconventional attack raised the spirits of colonists.

Who Were the Hessians?

The Hessians were approximately 30,000 professional soldiers from Germany who were hired by the British to fight on their side in the American Revolution. At the end of the war, some 3,000 Hessians decided that they quite liked this place they'd been fighting in and decided to stay in America rather than return to Europe.

2020 • *Soul*, the first Pixar movie featuring a Black leading character, premieres. The flick, about a middle school band teacher who longs to be a great jazz musician, wins two Oscars for Best Animated Feature and Best Original Score.

1946 — Mobster Bugsy Siegel opens the Flamingo Hotel in Las Vegas, hoping to make the city a glitzy, fancy-schmancy destination. His plan failed in the short term (the opening was a flop and his mob partners killed him because they thought he was stealing money) but succeeded in the long term, as the Flamingo is the oldest operating casino on the fabulous Las Vegas strip.

2004 — A massive earthquake off the coast of Indonesia creates a tsunami that brings utter devastation all along the Indian Ocean coastline. Waves as high as 100 feet wiped out highly populated areas in a dozen countries, including India, Indonesia, the Maldives, Sri Lanka, and Thailand, causing an estimated 230,000 deaths. The world responded to the disaster with historic fundraisers, donating $7 billion in funds to aid recovery.

1991 — **The Soviet Union comes to an end.** Created after the 1917 Russian Revolution that overthrew Russia's rulers, the Soviet Union or Union of Soviet Socialist Republics was a collection of Communist-controlled countries. It collapsed after decades of economic failure and mistrust in its political system. USSR leader Mikhail S. Gorbachev resigned, and the Soviet red flag with a hammer and sickle was lowered and replaced with the white-blue-red flag, representing the country of Russia, over the Kremlin.

DECEMBER 27

1904 — We can fly! **The play _Peter Pan_, written by J.M. Barrie, opens at the Duke of York's Theater in London.** It dazzled and inspired the audiences...a little too much. Barrie had to add "fairy dust" to the script as a necessary ingredient for the characters to fly because too many kids were heading home after the show and jumping off high things to see if they could fly too.

1932 — Thousands of people show up for the opening of Radio City Music Hall in New York City. The stunning art deco theater was designed to be a beautiful place where ordinary people could see extraordinary entertainment. An estimated 300 million audience members have taken in shows there, seeing everything from the premiere of _King Kong_ to legendary concerts to the _Christmas Spectacular_ featuring the high-kicking Rockettes.

DECEMBER 28

1922 — *Bam! Pow!* **It's the birthday of Stan Lee**, the comic book mastermind, who along with artists like Jack Kirby and Steve Ditko invented Marvel's most legendary heroes and villains, including Spider-Man, the Hulk, the X-Men, the Avengers, Black Panther, the Green Goblin, and Dr. Doom. We could keep listing the characters he co-created, but this book is starting to run out of room!

2008 — The Detroit Lions end their perfect NFL season—just not the kind you'd want. They went 0-16, making them the first team to lose every single game in the regular season.

? Did You Know?

Stan Lee made a cameo (small appearance) in all 22 movies in the MCU before his death in 2018.

DECEMBER 29

1890 — **The U.S. Army's Seventh Cavalry surrounds a band of Sioux near Wounded Knee Creek, South Dakota.** As the troops demanded that the Sioux surrender their weapons, a fight broke out, and a shot was fired. No one knows who fired it, but it launched an all-out attack, where an estimated 150 of the Sioux, including women and children, were killed. Originally described as a battle, today the Wounded Knee Massacre is remembered as a terrible and avoidable loss of human life.

2016 — In retaliation for Russian hackers trying to influence the outcome of the 2016 presidential election between Hillary Clinton and Donald Trump, President Barack Obama kicks 35 Russians out of the country.

DECEMBER 30

1803 • **After President Thomas Jefferson closes a $15 million deal with France, the United States completes the Louisiana Purchase.** This massive section of land stretched from the Mississippi to the Rocky Mountains and down to New Orleans. With that single purchase, the size of the United States instantly doubled.

A Great Day to Play

Happy birthday to two of arguably the greatest athletes to ever play their sports: Lebron James (1984) and Tiger Woods (1975). If today is also your birthday, congrats! It seems like you have pretty good odds of landing a billion-dollar contract in your favorite sport.

DECEMBER 31

1907 • **For the first time, a ball drops in Times Square to ring in the New Year.** The first ball was made of iron and wood and covered in 100 light bulbs. It was five feet in diameter and weighed 700 pounds. If you see this ball heading for you, do not try to catch it!

1912 • At age 11, Louis Armstrong is arrested for shooting a pistol into the air during a New Year's Eve celebration in New Orleans. He is sent to a reform school, where under the tutelage of the band instructor, he learns to play the coronet. Louis grows up to be a legendary jazz artist and one of the most famous performers in the world, whose songs include "What a Wonderful World."

1935 • Pass go and collect $200! On this day, **the classic board game Monopoly is patented.** If you've ever tried to play this game from beginning to end, you know that there is a good chance that the first game started in 1935 is still being played.

THIS DAY IN *my* HISTORY
DECEMBER

Fill in any memorable events from your life here.

1
2
3
4
5
6
7
8
9
10
11
12
13
14
15
16

17
18
19
20
21
22
23
24
25
26
27
28
29
30
31

INDEX

AIDS Memorial Quilt, 169
Aircraft, first sustained flight, 211
Alaska, sale of, 172
Alcatraz, 129
Antarctica facts, 20
Apes, humans and, 58, 212
Apple Computer, 57
Arbor Day, 61
Art class, world's largest, 37
Asian American and Pacific Islander
   Heritage Month, 73
Assassinations, 63, 103, 122, 144, 194
Astley, Philip, 12
ATM, first, 103
Atomic bombs, 123, 127

"Baby Shark" video, 182
Baker, Josephine, 164
Balloon flights. *See* Hot-air balloon
   flights
Baseball milestones/firsts, 30, 60, 64,
   69, 75, 81, 88, 125, 133, 135, 137, 160,
   163, 165, 166, 175, 189
Basketball, origin, 213
Batman, 55
Bermuda Triangle, 204
Bicycle, first, 94
Bifocals, invention, 84
Biles, Simone, 121
Black History Month, 25
Blackout, power, 131
Black Power salute, 171
Black Tuesday, 178
Black Wall Street riot, 88
Bly, Nellie, 168
Boston Massacre, 43
Bowling, first perfect game (300), 46
Boxers, 70, 151, 193
Boy Scouts of America, 29
Braille, Louis, 10
Bridges
   Brooklyn Bridge, 85
   first suspension bridge, 23
   Golden Gate Bridge, 10
   longest sea bridge-tunnel system,
     175
   longest suspension bridge, 193
   Verrazano Narrows Bridge, 193

Cannon, woman shot out of, 57
Capone, Al, 129, 172
Cars
   best-selling (VW Beetle), 34
   first Model T, 159
   first solar-powered, 139
   first speeding ticket, 22
   Ford Mustang, 65
   racing milestones, 45, 82, 88
Cartoon, first animated, 132
Carver, George Washington, 113
Cash register, invention, 183
Castrission, James, and Justin Jones, 14
Cats musical debut, 167

Cave paintings (Lascaux, France), 149
Cerebral palsy phenom, 138
Chamberlain, Wilt, 42
Channel Tunnel (Chunnel), 76
Charlotte's Web (White), 171
Chess champions, 30, 141
Chimpanzee artist, 99
Christmas Carol (Dickens), 212
Christmas Truce, 215
Cinco de Mayo, 75
Circus highlights, 12, 57, 90, 154
Civil Rights Act, 107
Comaneci, Nadia, 115
Computer, first (ENIAC), 32
Concorde jet flight, 18
Confucius, 160
Constitution. *See* U.S. Constitution
Cooper, Dan, 195
Copernicus, Nicolaus, 35
Copperfield, David, 60
Coral structure, Great Barrier Reef, 173
Cow (Ollie), first to fly in airplane, 34
Cryonics, first treatment, 14
CT scan, 163
Cuban Missile Crisis, 174
Curie, Marie, 208

Dalí, Salvidor, 78
Darwin, Charles, 151
Declaration of Independence, 108
Desilu Productions, 186
Devils Tower, 157
Diana, Princess of Wales, 139
Disability Pride Month, 106
Disney movies and Disneyland, 27, 44,
   115, 197, 213
DNA structure, discovered, 39
Dollar, naming of, 109
Dolly the sheep clone, 109
Douglass, Frederick, 25, 142
Dracula (Stoker) and Dracula, 186
Dragon, baby, 77
Drive-in movie theater, first, 92
Duel, Burr and Hamilton, 112
Dynamite, patent, 76

Earhart, Amelia, 83
Earth Day, 67
Easter Island, 59
Eclipse, solar, 118
Eiffel Tower, 55
Einstein, Albert, 48, 122
Endangered species list, 46
Erie Canal, 176
ESPN launched, 145
Euro, public circulation, 8

Falkland Islands, war, 50
Fantasmagorie, 132
Ferris Wheel invention, 100
Flag of United States, 95
Flying-trapeze act, first, 188
Football without helmets, 184
Franklin, Benjamin, 84, 85, 94, 120, 152
Freedom Tower, 70, 182
Friends (TV show) debut, 155

Gandhi, Mohandas, hunger strike, 152

Gettysburg Address, 192
Gettysburg, battle of, 107
Girl Scouts, 47
Globe theater burns, 104
Gold rushes, 20, 132
Goodall, Jane, 58
Grand Canyon, 38
Grauman's Chinese Theatre, 82
Groundhog Day, 26
Gulf War, 16, 125

Hailstones, 71
Halloween, 179
Harris, Kamala, 18
Heisman trophy, first, 207
Hispanic Heritage Month, 151
HMS *Beagle*, 151
Hockey facts, 36, 37, 43, 171, 196
Horses
   famed equestrian show opens, 12
   photos proving all feet airborne, 96
   Triple Crown winner Secretariat, 93
Hot-air balloon flights, 11, 51, 91, 174
Houdini, Harry, 154
Hudson, Henry, and Hudson River, 143

Ides of March, 48
Incredible Hulk, 73
Indian Removal Act, 87
Indigenous People's Day, 169
Integration of schools, 149, 189
International Day of Friendship, 123
Internet, origins, 71
Iron Lady, Africa's, 16

James, Jesse, 32
Jet-pack flight, 66
Joan of Arc, 71
Johnson, Dwayne "the Rock," 191
Johnson, Robert, 194
Jordan, Michael, 63, 64, 178
Juice box, origins, 60
Juneteenth, origins, 98

K-9 Corps, 47
Kennedy, John F., 94, 144, 158, 174, 194
King abdicating English throne, 208
King, Martin Luther, Jr., 53, 137, 182, 201
Knievel, Evel, 176
Knighthood, first actor to receive, 85
Kodak camera, 143
Kon-Tiki raft, 70

Labor Day, 144
Leaning Tower of Pisa, 11
Leap Day, 39
Lee, Bruce, 197
Lee, Stan, 218
LEGOLAND, first, 92
Liberty Bell, 110
Life origins on earth, 173
Light bulb, first, 17
Lincoln, Abraham, 8, 25, 62, 63, 83, 144,
   157, 165, 192
Lindow Man, 125
Lin, Jeremy, 135
Live Aid concert, 113
Lone Ranger, 23

(continued)

Lord of the Rings Trilogy (Tolkien), 122
Louisiana Purchase, 219
Lucy, ancient human remains of, 195
Luther, Martin, 179

Machu Picchu, 97, 119
Magicians and magic tricks, 16, 107
Malala Day, 112
Mandela, Nelson, 31
Man-made Wonders of the World, 97
Marceau, Marcel, 51
Mardi Gras, first parade, 39
Mark of Zorro (movie), 197
Marshall, Thurgood, 138
Mary Celeste, ship mystery, 204
Metallica band record performance, 207
Meteorites, 12, 69, 160, 199
Michelangelo, 44, 181
Microsoft, 58
Microwave oven, patent, 167
Miracle on the Hudson, 15
Monopoly game, patent, 219
Montezuma and Aztec treasures, 104
Motel, first in the world, 209
Mother Teresa, 147
Mount Everest, climbing, 79, 85, 88
Mount Rushmore, 165
Mummy of King Tut, 33
Mummy's voice, hearing, 19

NAACP, founding of, 31
National days
    Backward Day, 23
    Burrito Day, 60
    Chocolate Chip Cookie Day, 126
    Clean Up Your Room Day, 78
    Crayon Day, 55
    Doughnut Day, 183
    Fast-Food Day, 190
    First Responders Day, 177
    Girl Scout Day, 47
    Gummi Worm Day, 114
    Hot Dog Day, 116
    Ice Cream Sandwich Day, 125
    Junk Food Day, 117
    Librarian Day, 58
    Mac & Cheese Day, 113
    Meatball Day, 45
    Megalodon Day, 96
    Nachos Day, 184
    Pancake Day, 41
    Paper Airplane Day, 86
    Pizza Day, 30
    Popcorn Day, 17
    Rescue Dog Day, 83
    7-Eleven Day, 112
    S'Mores Day, 129
    Spaghetti Day, 10
    Taco Day, 165
    Teacher's Day, 74
    Tell a Joke Day, 132
    Tooth Fairy Day, 134
    Video Games Day, 149
National monument, first, 157
National Public Radio (NPR), 74
Native American Heritage Month, 181
Native American inventions, 181

Netflix, origins, 138
Newton, Isaac, 29
Niagara Falls, barrel rider surviving, 175
Niagara Falls, battle of, 120
9/11 attacks, 148
Nixon, Richard M., 128, 158
North Pole exploration, 59, 62, 90, 126
Nuclear power plant, first, 213
NYSE (New York Stock Exchange), 45

Oakley, Annie, 130
Olympics, first modern, 59
Olympics, Jamaican bobsleigh team, 38
One World Trade Center, 182
Oregon Trail, 84
Owens, Jesse, 128

Panda birth at National Zoo, 134
Paper dresses, 50
Paralympic Games, first, 153
Parks, Rosa, 201
PBS, origins, 166
Pearl Harbor attack, 206
Penguin Day, 69
Penicillin, discovery of, 160
Phonautograph, 61
Phone call, first international, 158
Picasso, Pablo, 101
Pi Day, 48
Pirates, female, 198
Plagues and quarantines, 121
Polk, westward expansion and, 202
Prehistoric humans, 47, 125, 195, 212
Presidential debate, first televised, 158
Presley, Elvis, 146
Prohibition, 177
Public enemy number one, first, 100

Railroad, longest, 117
Rainbow, longest lasting, 199
Random Acts of Kindness Day, 34
"Rapper's Delight" (Sugar Hill Gang), 152
Reagan, Ronald, 18, 52, 100 , 144, 182
Robinson, Jackie, 64
Rocky (movie), 193
Roller coaster, first, 96
Roller ("rocker") skate, patent, 11
Roosevelt, Theodore, 144, 157, 165, 189
Rosetta stone, 116
Round-the-world "drive," 79
Route 66, origins, 187

Same-sex marriage rights, 80
Saturday Evening Post covers by
    Rockwell, 83
Scooby-Doo TV debut, 150
Scotland Yard, origins, 161
Sesame Street, premiere of, 187
Shakespeare plays, 22, 104
Sherlock Holmes, origin, 201
Sign language, first international day
    of, 156
Sirleaf, Ellen Johnson, 16
Sistine Chapel ceiling, 181
Skateboarding, 53, 79, 118
Slavery, abolition of, 23
Soap box derby, 133
South Pole, 20, 62, 208, 210

Space exploration
    big bang and, 181
    black holes, 122, 205
    constellations list, 74
    earth's cousin discovered, 118
    earth-size diamond star, 101
    first American woman in space, 98
    first liquid-fuel rocket launch, 49
    first space selfie, 188
    first spacewalk, 28
    first stars' light detected, 181
    flyby to Comet Wild 2, 9
    flying saucers and, 110
    Halley's comet, 136
    hitting asteroid to change direction,
        159
    Hubble Space Telescope, 69
    Huygens lands on Titan (Saturn
        moon), 14
    Ingenuity helicopter on Mars, 66
    International Space Station, 26, 70,
        88, 91, 166, 202
    interstellar travel, 136
    John Glenn returns to space, 178
    long, long-distance message to star
        cluster, 190
    Mir space station, 35, 51, 104
    moon firsts (landings, information,
        etc.), 9, 26, 117, 123, 134
    moon, last landing, 209
    Outer Space Treaty, 168
    Pluto reclassified as dwarf planet,
        135
    rocket piece hitting citizen, 19
    SpaceX's first launch, 28
    A Trip to the Moon (film), 141
Spanish flu, 31
Spider-Man, 54, 129
SpongeBob SquarePants, 73
Spy equipment, 110, 125, 126, 133, 174
Squid (giant), first images of, 161
Star Trek, premiere of, 146
Statue of Liberty, 55, 60, 97
Stem cells, isolation of, 183
St. Patrick's Day parade, 49
Stranger Things series release, 87
Straw (drinking), patent, 9
Streetcars, electric, 79
Suez Canal, boat stuck in, 52
Summer solstice, 100
Superman, 55, 65
Supermarket, first, 144
Supernova, brightest, 71
Surfing backflip, 80

Table tennis, patent, 114
Taj Mahal construction, 97
Tallest man in history, 36
Telephone, invention, 44
Tennis matches, 22, 101, 114, 154, 163, 171
Tesla, Nicola, electricity and, 81
Text message, first, 203
Thatcher, Margaret, 75
Tightrope walk, World Trade Center, 127
Times Square New Year ball, 219
Time travelers' party, 103
Titanic, remains of, 141
Toaster, patent, 172

222

Toilet bowl theft, 150
Toilet paper, patent, 214
Toothbrush, patent, 102
Tour de France, first, 116
Toy Story (movie), 194
Traffic light, first, 127
Trains
    first steam-powered, 36
    high-speed test, 67
    largest underground system (NYC
      subway), 177
    Orient Express, 165
Tree, world's tallest, 136
Trojan War, 68
Tug-of-war in Olympics, 133
TV, development landmarks, 21, 53, 106,
  196
Tweed, William M. "Boss," 203
Twilight Zone, premiere of, 164
Twitter, start of, 51
Two dollar ($2) bills, 102
Typhoid Mary, 54
Tyrannosaurus rex, 130

Uncle Sam, origins, 145
U.N. Day of Happiness, 50
United Nations called to order, 13
U.S. Constitution
    Bill of Rights, 210
    Electoral College, 11
    electoral votes and, 11, 185
    "equal protection" clause, 122
    origins, 85, 152
    presidential term limit, 23
    same-sex marriage and, 80
    segregation and, 81
    three branches of government and,
      157
    voting rights, 57, 80, 133
U.S. postal system, origin, 120
U.S. Supreme Court, 80, 107, 128, 138,
  149, 157, 158, 185, 201

Van Gogh, Vincent, 214
Very Hungry Caterpillar (Carle), 91
Veterans Day, 187
Video games, 43, 84, 90, 111, 149, 156, 167,
  191, 198
Vietnam Veterans Memorial, 189
Viking Age of Conquest, 93
Volcano eruptions, 63, 82, 135, 137, 211
Voting rights. *See* U.S. Constitution
Voting rights, women in New Zealand,
  153

Wagon train first, 84
War of the Worlds (Wells), 178
Washington, George, 11, 14, 36, 71, 85, 95,
  108, 120, 127, 135, 165, 216
Wendy's restaurant, first, 190
White House, cornerstone, 170
Winnie-the-Pooh (Milne), 170
Witchcraft, 155
Women's History Month, 41
Wonderful Wizard of Oz (Baum), 81
Wonder Woman, 174
Woods, Tiger, 63, 219
Woodstock music festival, 131

World Cups, 50, 95, 111
World Religion Day, 15
World War II (WW II)
    Aztec Eagles Squadron, 119
    candy rationing, 27
    combatant found 28 years after, 20
    great escape from prison camp, 52
    Holocaust and Auschwitz liberation,
      21
    Iwo Jima flag raised, 37
    Japan's surrender, 142
    Marshall Plan, 92
    Rosie the Riveter poster, 33
    "scrap days" for metal, 165
    sliced bread ban, 17
    VE Day, 77
World War I (WWI), 31, 67, 76, 103, 122,
  152, 187, 208, 215
World Wildlife Day, 43
Wounded Knee Massacre, 218
Wright, Orville and Wilbur, 211

X-rays, first used, 13

Yellowstone National Park, 14, 41
YouTube, origins, 68
Yo-yo, invention, 192

CREDITS

Book design and illustrations by Russell Shaw

Library of Congress Cataloging-in-Publication Data available on request
10 9 8 7 6 5 4 3 2

Published by Hearst Home Kids, an imprint of Hearst Books/Hearst Communications, Inc.
300 W 57th Street
New York, NY 10019

For information about custom editions, special sales, premium and corporate purchases: hearst.com/magazines/hearst-books

Printed in China
ISBN 978-1-958395-79-0